W9-AXU-035

Unbelievably Good Deals and Great Adventures That You Absolutely Can't Get Unless You're Over

50

Unbelievably Good Deals and Great Adventures That You Absolutely Can't Get Unless You're Over

50

JOAN RATTNER HEILMAN

CB

CONTEMPORARY BOOKS

Library of Congress Cataloging-in-Publication Data
is available from the United States Library of Congress.

Cover design by Kim Bartko
Interior design by Terry Stone

Published by Contemporary Books
An imprint of NTC/Contemporary Publishing Group, Inc.
4255 West Touhy Avenue, Lincolnwood (Chicago), Illinois 60646-1975 U.S.A.
Copyright © 1998, 1997, 1996, 1995, 1994, 1993, 1992, 1990, 1989, 1988
by Joan Rattner Heilman
All rights reserved. No part of this book may be reproduced, stored in a retrieval
system, or transmitted in any form or by any means, electronic, mechanical,
photocopying, recording, or otherwise, without the prior permission of
NTC/Contemporary Publishing Group, Inc.
Printed in the United States of America
International Standard Book Number: 0-8092-2894-7

18   17   16   15   14   13   12   11   10   9   8   7   6   5   4   3   2

Contents

Unbelievably Good Deals and Great Adventures That You Absolutely Can't Get Unless You're Over

50

1

Introduction to Good Deals and Great Adventures

This book is for people who love to do interesting things and go to new places—and don't mind saving money while they're at it. It is a guide to the perks, privileges, discounts, and special adventures to which you have become entitled simply because you've been around for 50 years or more.

On your 50th birthday (or on your 60th, 62nd, or 65th), you qualify for hundreds of special opportunities and money-saving offers that have lots of younger people wishing they were older—all for a couple of good reasons. First, as a person in your prime, you deserve them.

Second, as part of the fastest-growing segment of the American population, you represent an enormous market of potential consumers, a fact that has become quite apparent to the business community. More than a quarter of the U.S. population today is over 50; by 2020 that pro-

1

portion will increase to a third as the first wave of 77 million baby boomers turns 50. About 34 million Americans—1 in 8—are now over 65, and it is estimated that by 2030 this group will increase to more than twice that number. Besides, life expectancy is higher today than ever before, and most of us can expect to live a long, healthy, and active life.

Those of us over 50 control most of the nation's wealth, including half of the discretionary income, the money that's left over after essentials have been taken care of, and almost 80 percent of its financial assets. Very often, the children have gone, the mortgage has been paid off, the house is fully furnished, the goal of leaving a large inheritance is not a major concern, and the freedom years have arrived at last.

As a group, we're markedly different from previous older generations who pinched pennies and saved them all. We, too, know the value of a dollar, but we feel freer to spend our money because we're better off than our predecessors, a significant number of us having accumulated enough resources to be reasonably secure. We also are far better educated than those before us, and we have developed many more interests and activities.

And, most important, we as a group are remarkably fit, healthy, and energetic. We are in *very* good shape—and feel that way. In fact, a survey has shown that most of us feel at least 15 years younger than our chronological age.

The business community is actively courting the mature market, as we are known, because now many of us have the time and the money to do all the things we've always put off. Because of the recognition of our numbers, our flexible schedules, and our vast buying power, we are finally being taken very seriously. To get our attention, we are increasingly presented with some real breaks and good deals, all detailed on these pages. We are also invited on trips and adventures specifically tailored to suit our interests, needs, and abilities.

In this book, you will learn how to get what's coming to you—the discounts and privileges you absolutely couldn't get if you were younger:

■ Discounts at hotels and motels, at car-rental agencies, on buses, trains, and boats
■ Price breaks on airfares from virtually all airlines
■ Colleges and universities that offer you an education at bargain rates
■ Insurance companies with discounts for people at 50 or thereabouts
■ Travel adventures all over the world designed specifically for older travelers
■ Clubs, trips, and services for mature singles
■ Ski resorts where you can ski for half price—or for nothing
■ Tennis tournaments, golf vacations, walking trips, bike tours, and senior softball leagues designed for you
■ And much more!

Because every community has its own special perks to offer you, make a practice of *asking* if there are breaks to which you are entitled wherever you go, from movies to museums, concerts to historic sites, hotels to ski resorts, restaurants to riverboats, in this country and abroad. Don't expect clerks or ticket agents, tour operators, restaurant hosts, even travel agents to volunteer them to you. First of all, they may not think of it. Second, they may not realize you have reached the appropriate birthday. And third, they may not want to call attention to your age, just in case that's not something you would appreciate! You never know if you're being offered the best possible deal unless you ask. Many bargains and privileges are available only to people who speak up.

Remember to request your privileges *before* you pay or when you order or make reservations, and always carry proof of age or an over-50-club membership card, or, better yet, both. Sometimes the advantages come with membership in a senior club, but usually they are available to anyone over a specified age.

To make sure you're getting a legitimate discount when you want to take advantage of your over-50 privileges away from home, call the hotel, airline, car-rental company, or tour operator and ask what the regular or normal prices are. Find out if there's a special sale going on. Then decide whether you are getting a good deal. And, most important, always ask for *the lowest available rate* at the time you plan to travel and compare that with your discounted rate. Sometimes you'll find that even better specials are available.

With the help of this guidebook, completely revised and updated at least once a year, you will have a wonderful time and save money too.

2

Travel: Making Your Age Pay Off

People over 50 are the most ardent travelers of all. We travel more often, farther, more extravagantly, and for longer periods of time than anybody else. Ever since the travel industry discovered these facts, it's been after our business.

It's fallen in love with our age group because we have more discretionary income than people of other ages and more time to spend it. Besides, we are remarkably flexible. Many of us no longer have children in school, so we're free to travel at off-peak times or whenever we feel the need for a change of scenery. In fact, we much prefer spring and fall to summer. Some of us have retired, and others have such good jobs that we can make our own schedules. We can take advantage of midweek or weekend slack times when the industry is eager to fill space.

But, best of all, we are energetic, and we're not about to stay home too much. People over 50 account for about one-third of all domestic travel, air trips, hotel/motel nights, and trips to Europe and Africa. Nine out of ten of us are experienced travelers and savvy consumers.

Contrary to what a younger person might think, people in the mature generation aren't content with watching the action. Instead, we like to get right into the middle of it. There's not a place we won't go or an activity we won't try. Though many of us prefer escorted tours, almost half of us choose to travel independently.

Not only that, but we're shrewd—we look for the best deals to the best places. We are experienced comparison shoppers and seek the most for our money.

For all these reasons, we are now offered astonishing numbers of travel-related discounts and reduced rates as well as special tour packages and other perks. Many agencies and tour operators have designed all or at least part of their trips for a mature clientele. Others include older travelers with everyone else but offer us special privileges.

Most airlines sell senior coupon books, good for a year, that let us travel much more cheaply than other people or, instead, give those of us over 62 a 10 percent reduction on regular fares. And practically all hotel and motel chains— as well as individual establishments—now offer similar inducements, such as discounts on rooms and restaurants.

There are so many good deals and great adventures available to you when you are on the move that we'll start right off with travel.

But, first, keep in mind:

■ Rates, trips, and privileges tend to change at a moment's notice, so check out each of them before you make your plans. Airlines and car-rental agencies are particularly capricious, and it's hard to tell what they offer from one week to the next. The good deals in this guidebook are those that are available as we go to press.

■ Always ask for your discount when you make your reservations or at the time of purchase, order, or check-in. If you wait until you're checking out or settling your bill, it may be too late.

■ Also remember that discounts may apply only between certain hours, on certain days of the week, or during specific seasons of the year. Research this before making reservations and always remind the clerk of the discount when you check in or pay your fare. Be flexible when you can and travel during the hours, days, or seasons when you can get the best deals.

■ It's particularly important when traveling to carry identification with proof of age or membership in a senior club. In most cases, a driver's license or passport does the job. So, in some cases, does the organization's membership card, a birth certificate, a resident alien card, or any other official document showing your date of birth. If you're old enough for a Medicare card or Senior ID card, use that.

■ Don't always spring for the senior discount without checking out other rates. Sometimes special promotional rates or discounts available to anybody any age turn out to be better deals. The car-rental companies and rail-roads, for example, are famous for this. Ask your travel agent or the ticket seller to figure out the *lowest possible available rate* for you at that moment.

■ Some of these bargains are yours at age 50, usually but not always tied to membership in a senior organization. Others come along a little later at varying birthdays, so watch for the cutoff points. Also, in most cases, if the person purchasing the ticket or trip is the right age, the rest of the party, a traveling companion, or the people sharing the room are entitled to the same reduced rates.

3

Out-of-the-Ordinary Escapades

If you are an intrepid, energetic, perhaps even courageous sort of person who's intrigued by adventures that don't tempt the traditional travelers, take a look at these unusual vacation suggestions, all of them planned specifically for the mature population. They are certain to give you tales with which to entertain your friends, relatives, and acquaintances—at least until your next adventure.

ALASKA WILDLAND ADVENTURES

AWA's Senior Safaris are adventure tours designed specifically for energetic mature travelers who are looking for action and can move right along but don't want to worry about keeping up with 30-somethings. Several 7- and 9-day senior trips are offered in the summer months, during which AWA also has similar but more ambitious ecotours for all ages. The itinerary, planned to accommodate all levels of ability and stamina, gives you a glimpse of Alaska up close as you raft down the Kenai River; travel by yacht in Prince William Sound to watch whales, sea otters, glaciers, and birds; travel north to tour national parks and refuges; hike in forests and across the tundra; visit historic bushtowns; and view grizzly bears, moose, and other wild creatures.

Among other lodgings, your group stays at a comfortable motel in Kenai and the Denali Backcountry Lodge in Denali National Park, always with your own private bathroom. Mention your membership in a recognized senior organization, and you will get a $50 discount.

For information: Alaska Wildland Adventures, PO Box 389, Girdwood, AK 99587; 800-334-8730.

AMERICAN WILDERNESS EXPERIENCE

If you love adventurous vacations and roughing it in style, study the many offerings from AWE, an agency that's spent many years sending travelers on backcountry wilderness adventures and taking care of all the details. Its offerings are gathered from many tour operators and are open to all ages, but some are specifically designed for over-50s, and a few give discounts to seniors. Among these are a canoe trip in the Boundary Waters between Minnesota and Ontario, senior safaris in Alaska, horseback trips in Colorado or New Mexico, and a mountain sports week that combines rock climbing, horseback riding, mountain biking, and whitewater rafting in Colorado. Other trips feature special departures and itineraries for prime timers.

For information: American Wilderness Experience, PO Box

1486, Boulder, CO 80306; 800-444-0099 or 303-444-2622.

ARIZONA RAFT ADVENTURES

The Senior Archaeology Tour offered by AZRA takes you on a 3- or 4-day, 27-mile raft trip down the upper San Juan River in the southwestern corner of Utah to visit some of the areas inhabited by the Anasazi Indians hundreds of years ago. While exploring the sites along the river and hearing interpretive talks about Anasazi culture, you'll see ancient ruins, artifacts, petroglyphs, pioneer trails, geological phenomena, and abundant wildlife. You'll travel in a rubber raft rowed by a guide, take some hikes, spend the nights at campsites on the sandy riverbanks, and enjoy the company of a small group from your own generation.

For information: Arizona Raft Adventures, 4050 E. Huntington Drive, Flagstaff, AZ 86004; 800-786-7238 or 520-526-8200.

GREAT ALASKA SAFARIS

The Silver Safaris, scheduled several times a summer, were created expressly for older travelers who want comfort as well as adventure. Mellower than trips planned for all ages, the seven-day safaris start at the Great Alaska Fish Camp on the Kenai Peninsula, where you stay in riverside cabins and take a trip to Homer, a remote artists' community. After hikes and other adventures, plus a glacier and wildlife cruise in Prince William Sound and a visit to Anchorage, you fly to a wilderness camp in Lake Clark National Park to view bears, moose, and other creatures of the wild.

For information: Great Alaska Safaris, HC01, Box 218, Sterling, AK 99672; 800-544-2261.

HOSTELLING INTERNATIONAL/ AMERICAN YOUTH HOSTELS

This organization is probably best known for its low-cost bike and backpack trips for teenagers, but, in fact, it welcomes people of all ages. Once you become a member, you may participate in any of its "open" or "adult" adventures and book lodgings at the nearly 5,000 remarkably inexpensive HI hostels in more than 70 countries. Membership for adults costs $25 a year, but if you've reached the age of 55 you pay only $15. You will get a membership card, a guidebook listing 150 hostels in the United States and 80 in Canada, and access to all affiliated hostels worldwide.

The hostels vary from a castle in Germany to a lighthouse in California, a former dude ranch in Colorado, and a base camp in the Alps. Most hostels have kitchens where you prepare your own meals, and a few have cafeterias.

Members may stay at any hostel in the world, including the network of urban hostels located in Washington, D.C., New York, Boston, Pittsburgh, San Francisco, Orlando, Miami Beach, New Orleans, Los Angeles, San Diego, and Honolulu. One night's stay costs $8 to $24. There is no maximum age limitation for booking a bed in these wonderfully cheap lodgings and hobnobbing with other hostelers who prefer not to pay exorbitant hotel prices. Be ready, however, to sleep in a double-decker cot in a sex-segregated dormitory for six or eight people supervised by "hostel parents." Many hostels have family or couple rooms, however, that can be reserved in advance.

For information: HI/AYH, Dept. 855, 733 15th St. NW, Ste. 840, Washington, DC 20005; 202-783-6161.

HOSTELLING INTERNATIONAL–CANADA

A network of hostels throughout the Canadian provinces, HI-Canada offers members of all ages an inexpensive night's sleep in a wide variety of places ranging from historic homes and refurbished jails and courthouses to log cabins in the mountains. Located in all major gateway cities and also in remote locations, your accommodations—shared, simple, and quite basic—cost an average of $15 (Canadian) a night. Membership costs $25 (Canadian) per year and allows you to use any HI facility worldwide.

For information: Hostelling International–Canada, 205 Catherine St., Ste. 400, Ottawa, ON K2P 1C3; 800-663-5717 (Canada only) or 613-237-7884.

MT. ROBSON ADVENTURE HOLIDAYS

For people over 50 who crave action and the wilderness, this agency plans a couple of "gentle adventures" every summer in British Columbia's Mt. Robson Provincial Park, just west of Jasper. Mt. Robson is the highest mountain in the Canadian Rockies, and the park offers spectacular scenery. The Fifty Plus Adventure is a five-night package trip for up to 14 participants that includes a guided trek, a nature tour, a marshlands canoe trip, and a gentle rafting float trip, all led by local naturalists. You sleep at the base camp in heated log cabins with private bathrooms and eat three hearty meals a day.

For information: Mt. Robson Adventure Holidays, PO Box 687, Valemount, BC V0E 2Z0; 250-566-4386.

OUTWARD BOUND

Famous for its wilderness trips to build self-confidence, self-esteem, and the ability to work as a team, Outward Bound offers short adventure education courses specifically for adults. A few of the courses, in fact, are limited to adults over 40 or 50 and are designed for adults "who want to examine their personal or career goals, gain insights, renew energies, and develop new skills." The physical activities are challenging, and participants are expected to push themselves beyond their self-imposed physical and mental limits.

The 5- to 14-day courses include backpacking in the southern Appalachians, canoeing, sailing off the Maine coast or in the Florida Keys, and backpacking in Maine or the Texas desert. You'll sleep in a tent or under a tarp and cook your own food. To participate, you must be in good health and average physical condition but you needn't be an experienced camper.

For information: Outward Bound USA, Route 9D, R2 Box 280, Garrison, NY 10524-9757; 800-243-8520.

OVERSEAS ADVENTURE TRAVEL

OAT's soft adventures exclusively for travelers over 50 combine creature comforts with off-the-beaten-path experiences in exotic places all over the world, from the rain forests of Borneo to Botswana or the Galapagos Islands. With groups of no more than 16, the trips—rated from "easy" to "demanding"—move along at a leisurely pace and offer many optional side adventures. You'll lodge in accommodations ranging from five-star hotels to jungle lodges, small inns, or spacious tents and sometimes use unconventional modes of transportation such as dugout canoes, camels, switchback trains, yachts, or your own two feet.

Among current tours, always including round-trip air, from this affiliate of Grand Circle Travel are excursions to the Amazon, Peru, Antarctica, Morocco, Nepal, China, and Turkey.

Solo travelers are not charged a single supplement if they are willing to share accommodations, even if a roommate has not been assigned.

For information: Overseas Adventure Travel, 625 Mt. Auburn St., Cambridge, MA 02138; 800-955-1925.

RIVER ODYSSEYS WEST

ROW reserves a couple of whitewater river trips each summer exclusively for adventurous people over 55 who like to travel with others their own age. These Prime Time trips take you down Idaho's Salmon River and the Snake River on the Oregon border for five days, passing through four spectacular volcanic canyons. You travel in rubber rafts by day and sleep in tents at the edge of the river by night.

Another choice for mature travelers is one of ROW's raft-supported walking trips in Hells Canyon or the Salmon River in Idaho. See Chapter 13 for details.

A third option for older travelers is a 12-day sea voyage along the southern coast of Turkey in a 72-foot motorsail yacht, with time for visits to villages, beaches, and ancient ruins.

For information: River Odysseys West, PO Box 579-UD, Coeur d'Alene, ID 83816 0579, 800-451-6034 or 208-765-0841.

WARREN RIVER EXPEDITIONS

Warren River Expeditions offers whitewater raft trips for seniors down Idaho's Salmon River, the longest undammed river in the country—fast and wild in the spring, tame and gentle in late summer. You'll float through unique ecosystems, down the deep Salmon River Canyon, and through the Frank Church Wilderness Area, where you'll view the lush scenery and the abundant wildlife. Planned as soft adventure trips for people who are not enthusiastic about sleeping on the ground, the six-day senior trips put you up each night in comfortable backcountry lodges. Want to take the trip with your grandchildren? There is a grandparent expedition at least twice every summer plus a 10 percent discount for those over 50 or under 16.

For information: Warren River Expeditions, PO Box 1375, Salmon, ID 83467-1375; 800-765-0421 or 208-756-6387.

TAKE A GRANDCHILD ON VACATION

Would you like to get to know your grandchildren better? Take them on vacation. A trip with the kids is a wonderful way to get close to them, especially for families who live many miles apart and seldom have a chance to get together. Whether it's a one-day tour of a nearby city or two weeks on a dude ranch, this is the kind of family togetherness that works. You can plan your own itineraries, maybe visiting places you both want to see, renting a cottage at the beach, or choosing a resort or cruise that offers special activities for the youngsters.

Or you can do it the easy way by deciding on a ready-made grandparent/grandchild vacation. Scheduled in the summer or during the usual winter school breaks, the best of the group tours are fully escorted by counselors, many of them schoolteachers on holiday. The tours, which range from a visit to Washington, D.C., to a safari in Kenya, go at a leisurely pace suitable to both generations with plenty of stops and time to relax and relate.

Growing in popularity too are other multigenerational holidays, such as adventures for mothers and grown daughters, hostelers and adult children, and whole families including children, parents, and grandparents. Here are some of the current choices for a vacation with the family.

AFC TOURS

Check out AFC's grandparent tours if you're looking for quality time with the children without the hassles of planning and traveling on your own. Scheduled during the summer holidays are one-week trips to Disney World and the Kennedy Space Center and visits to favorite U.S. cities, such as New York and Philadelphia, Boston, and Washington, D.C. The supervised program includes activities for both age groups and a tour manager to lead the way.

For information: AFC Tours, 11772 Sorrento Valley Rd., San Diego, CA 92121; 800-369-3693 or 619-481-8188.

AMERICAN MUSEUM OF NATURAL HISTORY FAMILY TOURS

This prestigious museum runs educational travel trips for children (17 and up) accompanied by parents or grandparents (or both). You and your grandchildren may choose to spend the winter holidays sailing aboard a clipper ship in the Caribbean and visiting six tropical islands. Or decide to take a trip to Ecuador and the Galapagos Islands, where you'll cruise among remote volcanic islands and make the acquaintance of the unique wildlife. Other choices for family tours include an Alaska wilderness and glacier exploration, and a winter safari to Kenya for close encounters with lions, elephants, and giraffes. Groups are led by museum naturalists.

For information: Discovery Tours, American Museum of Natural History, Central Park West at 79th St., New York, NY 10024; 800-462-8687 or 212-769-5700.

ELDERHOSTEL

Elderhostel, wildly popular among mature travelers for its hundreds of inexpensive residential learning programs, reserves special weeks for hostelers and their grandchildren or other young friends—and several for members and their adult children, such as the one for grandmothers and granddaughters ages 16 to 25 at the Victoria Inn in Ontario. Designed to give you time together unhassled by everyday pressures, the offerings change every season. Recent programs have included, for example, wagon-train trips through the Black Hills of South Dakota, a performing arts program in Massachusetts, a geology and wildflower exploration in the Colorado Rockies, and rock climbing, caving, and water ecology in a park in Kentucky.

For information: Elderhostel, 75 Federal St., Boston, MA 02110; 617-426-7788. In Canada: Elderhostel Canada, 5 Cataraqui St., Kingston, ON K7K 1Z7; 613-530-2222.

FAMILYHOSTEL

Foreign adventures are the specialty of FamilyHostel, an educational travel program sponsored by University of New Hampshire Continuing Education that takes families—perhaps you and your grandchildren (ages 8 to 15)—on 10-day summer trips to such places as France, England, and Switzerland. Separately and together, you attend classes, go on field trips, and enjoy recreational activities. Lodging is usually in university residence halls or apartments and the cost is moderate for what you get.

For information: FamilyHostel, University of New Hampshire, 6 Garrison Ave., Durham, NH 03824; 800-733-9753.

GRANDEXPLORERS

The twice-a-year, 10-day tours of Israel from GrandExplorers, a program created by B'nai B'rith, are designed to help grandparents pass on Jewish family heritage, values, and traditions to the younger generation. Included are stays in Jerusalem and Tel Aviv, a jeep tour of the Golan Heights, a camping trip with a Bedouin family for the children, camel rides, visits to historic sites throughout Israel, and two nights on a kibbutz.

For information: GrandExplorers, B'nai B'rith Israel Commission, 1640 Rhode Island Ave. NW, Washington, DC 20036; 800-500-6533 or 202-857-6577.

GRANDPARENTS' HOUSEPARTY

Choose from among more than 10,000 private homes—from cottages to castles—in England, Ireland, Scotland, or Wales, and take the kids along for a week or more. Country Cottages offers its Grandparents' Houseparty package that at some times of the year costs about $100 a day per person, including round-trip air from New York and a rental car or minivan, and in some seasons adds a small discount for grandparents and grandchildren. All of the properties are second homes equipped with linens, tableware, and cookware and have an accessible caretaker to provide information or assistance.

For information: Country Cottages, Box 810997, Boca Raton, FL 33481-0997; 800-674-8883.

GRANDTRAVEL

Grandtravel originated the idea of taking grandparents and their grandchildren off on vacation together. For grandparents any age and children aged 7 to 17, the tours include such adventures as visits to the Southwest Indian country, Alaska, or Ireland; barge trips in Holland; tours of famous castles in England and Scotland; and safaris in Kenya. If you want to go without a group, the agency will also arrange a special tour just for you. You don't have to be an authentic grandparent to take a trip—aunts, uncles, cousins, godparents, and other surrogate grandparents are welcome.

Tours, led by teacher-escorts, range from 7 to 18 days and always include time for both generations to spend time alone with their own age groups and plenty of rest stops. As part of its package, Grandtravel includes predeparture counseling to help you deal with any special concerns such as what to pack or how to deal with kids who miss their moms.

For information: Grandtravel, The Ticket Counter, 6900 Wisconsin Ave., Chevy Chase, MD 20815; 800-247-7651 or 301-986-0790.

GREAT CAMP SAGAMORE

Take your grandchild to camp with you for a week in August. The site is the Great Camp Sagamore, a former Vanderbilt wilderness retreat in New York State's Adirondack Park, and the purpose is to bring the two generations together to have fun and get to know one another better. Mornings, the campers engage in joint activities such as walks, berry picking, games, and nature art. Afternoons, the age groups are on their own, free to choose from options that include music, crafts, and swimming. Before dinner, grandparents meet for discussions of their own issues, and in the evenings everyone gets together for stories, campfires, sing-alongs, square dancing, and other activities.

For information: Great Camp Sagamore, Sagamore Rd., Raquette Lake, NY 13436; 315-354-5311.

IRISH FESTIVAL TOURS

For a visit to your Irish roots, gather up your grandchildren (or nieces, nephews, or other young friends) this summer and take them on a 10-day tour that includes Dublin, Avoca, Waterford, Killarney, the Ring of Kerry, and Galway. You'll learn about the folklore and traditions of the Irish people; visit castles, villages, farms, and museums; listen to storytellers; go pony trekking; see a working dairy farm; learn traditional dances; and otherwise enjoy a respite just for you and the grandkids. Most activities include both generations, but some separate events are planned as well.

For information: Irish Festival Tours, PO Box 169, Warminster, PA 18974; 800-441-4277.

RASCALS IN PARADISE

Specializing in family vacations for parents and children, Rascals in Paradise also invites grandparents and grandchildren to go along on its adventure trips to such places as Mexico and the Caribbean, the Bahamas, Europe, New Zealand, Thailand, Australia, the Canadian Rockies, Africa, the Galapagos Islands, Hawaii, Alaska, and ranches in the West. All group trips, three to six families per group, include escorts who plan activities for the older children and arrange baby-sitters for the little ones. This agency will plan independent vacations, too, as well as family reunions and other multigenerational celebrations.

For information: Rascals in Paradise, 650 Fifth St., Ste. 505, San Francisco, CA 94107; 800-872-7225 or 415-978-9800.

ROOTS & WINGS EXCURSIONS

Intergenerational travel is the specialty here. Among other family-oriented excursions, many trips are planned exclusively for grandparents and their grandchildren, and more just for mothers and their adult daughters. The GrandTrips include weekend adventures with other grandfamilies to such places as the Florida Keys, the Florida space coast, Amish country, and Civil War battlefields. Longer domestic journeys currently go to Hawaii, the Canadian Rockies, the Wild West, Alaska, and Chesapeake Bay. Abroad, destinations include the British Isles and Italy.

Mother & Daughter Discoveries are designed to allow mothers, daughters, and grandmothers to spend time together enjoying one another's company and special places such as the wine country of California, the antebellum South, Annapolis, New York City, and Bermuda.

For information: Roots & Wings Excursions, 423 Carlisle Dr., Herndon, VA 20170; 800-722-9005 or 703-834-7244.

SIERRA CLUB

A couple of remarkably inexpensive summertime vacations for grandparents and their grandchildren, led by experienced volunteers, are recent arrivals among the Sierra Club's famous outings. One of these outings is a laid-back and relaxed holiday, while the other is a rugged adventure recommended only for grandmas and grandpas in very good physical condition.

The first is a five-day stay at the Sierra Club's own rustic lodge near Donner Pass, in California's Sierra Nevadas. The outing is designed for people between 5 and 95, and all activities are optional. You lodge in rather spartan rooms, eat hearty meals, and enjoy yourselves doing such things as hiking, strolling, climbing to the top of Donner Peak, taking the tram to the top of Squaw Valley, having a picnic at Donner Lake, fishing, swimming, visiting historic sites, and singing around the campfire.

The more rigorous outing for the two generations is a four-day backpacking trip in California's Carson-Iceberg Wilderness. This one is definitely not for couch potatoes— grandparents must have previous backpacking experience and must be able to hike with full packs at high elevations. You'll hike to a base camp carrying your personal gear plus commissary gear and food, set up camp, help cook and clean up, and spend your days with the grandkids hiking, fishing, swimming, and exploring.

For information: Sierra Club Outing Dept., 85 Second St., San Francisco, CA 94105; 415-977-5522.

VISTA TOURS

This agency's family tours include two trips in the summer exclusively for grandparents and their children's children. The eight-day Western Adventure takes you and the kids by motorcoach to such intriguing places as Colorado Springs, Pike's Peak, Cheyenne, Casper, Medicine Bow, Mt. Rushmore, and Rocky Mountain National Park. The Florida Fun Tour, a 10-day adventure, settles you down in Orlando and then escorts you to Disney World, Epcott, MGM, Cypress Gardens, Kennedy Space Center, Cocoa Beach, and an alligator farm. Activities are planned for the two generations separately and together.

For information: Vista Tours, 1923 N. Carson St., Ste. 105, Carson City, NV 89701; 800-248-4782.

WARREN RIVER EXPEDITIONS

Take the kids down the Salmon River in Idaho on a raft trip run by Warren River Expeditions. You'll sleep in comfortable backcountry lodges along the river's edge and have plenty of exciting adventures on the big rubber rafts powered by expert oarspeople. Several special departures, with discounts for those over 50 or under 16, are reserved each summer for the two generations.

For information: Warren River Expeditions, PO Box 1375, Salmon, ID 83467-1375; 800-765-0421 or 208-756-6387.

4

Cutting Your Costs Abroad

The most enthusiastic voyagers of all age groups, Americans over 50—one out of three adults and a quarter of the total population—spend more time and money on travel than anybody else, especially when it comes to going abroad. It's been estimated that more than 4 out of every 10 passport holders are at least 55 years old. And there's hardly a country in the world today that doesn't actively encourage mature travelers to come for a visit, because everybody has discovered that they are travel's biggest potential market.

Because you are now being avidly pursued, you can take advantage of many good deals in other lands. Airlines, for example, often give you fare reductions on domestic flights within the country. Railroad systems in most European countries offer deep discounts to seniors that are especially valuable if you plan an extended stay in one place.

This chapter gives you a rundown on these and other ways to cut your European holiday costs, especially if you are planning your trip on your own. For the U.S. and Canada, see Chapter 9.

But, first, keep in mind:

■ Always ask about senior savings when you travel on trains, buses, or boats anywhere in the world. Do the same when you buy tickets for movies, theater, museums, tours, sightseeing sites, historic buildings, and attractions. Don't assume, simply because you haven't heard about them or the ticket agent hasn't mentioned them, that they don't exist. They are becoming more and more common everywhere.

■ Some countries require that you purchase a senior card to take advantage of senior discounts, but most require only proof of age, usually in the form of a passport.

■ Always have the necessary identification with you and be ready to show it. Occasionally you may need an extra passport photograph.

■ For specifics on a country's senior discounts, call its national tourist office.

■ Call Rail Europe (800-438-7245), which represents most European railways, for information about train passes.

■ Your passport may be required along with your rail pass while you are in transit, so keep it with you.

■ Rail passes, including many national passes, sold in the U.S. and Canada can be bought from any travel agency or directly from Rail Europe. The national passes are often available only at major rail stations or airports within a country. Be prepared to show your passport.

EUROPE BY RAIL

Rail passes make the going cheaper in Europe, especially if you travel with a companion or a group, and it's easier to use them than to buy tickets as you go. Besides, some of them offer senior discounts. It's not a simple matter to sort them all out, however. Some are multinational, good for travel in more than one country. Others are valid only within the borders of one country; these are usually designed for residents but useful to tourists as well. Most passes are available in two different versions: a flexipass that permits travel for a specified number of days within a certain time period, and a consecutive-day pass that is valid on any day within a certain period. Many are not available overseas and must be purchased on this side of the Atlantic before you go. Others may only be purchased in the country that issues them.

EURAILPASS AND EUROPASS

The Eurailpass gives you free unlimited first-class train travel in Hungary and on all the major railways of Western Europe except Great Britain's. There is no senior discount on this pass, but it is worth considering if you plan to cover many miles in many countries. On the other hand, if you are visiting just one country, you'd probably do better with that nation's senior discounts or national pass. Available for various numbers of days up to three months, the Eurailpass also entitles you to free or discounted travel on many buses, ferries, steamers, and suburban trains. If you are traveling with at least one other person, you can get a Eurail Saverpass or Eurail Saver Flexipass, which is an even better deal.

The Europass, less expensive, is another option. It is good for unlimited first-class train travel any time within a two-month period in five western European countries (France, Germany, Italy, Spain, and Switzerland). Other countries may be added with a surcharge.

None of these passes is sold in Europe and must be purchased before you leave home. And none gives seniors a special break.

For information: Rail Europe, 2100 Central Ave., Boulder, CO 80301; 800-4-EURAIL (800-438-7245).

FINDING A DOCTOR OVERSEAS

Before you leave on a trip to foreign lands, it would be wise to send for IAMAT's list of physicians all over the world who speak English or French, have had medical training in Great Britain, the U.S., or Canada, and have agreed to reasonable preset fees. When you join the free nonprofit **International Association for Medical Assistance to Travellers** (IAMAT), you will get a membership card entitling you to services and its prearranged rates, a directory of physicians in 125 countries and territories, a clinical record to take along with you, and advice on immunizations and preventive measures. Information about climate, food, water, and sanitary conditions in 450 cities is given to members who donate $25 or more. *For information:* IAMAT, 417 Center St., Lewiston, NY 14092; 716-754-4883.

SCANRAIL 55+ PASS

Sold only on this side of the Atlantic, Scanrail gives you unlimited travel in Denmark, Finland, Norway, and Sweden. If you're over 55, buy the Scanrail 55+ Pass, giving you the

same privileges, but for less than younger adults pay. For details, see Scandinavian Countries later in this chapter.
For information: Rail Europe, 2100 Central Ave., Boulder, CO 80301; 800-4-EURAIL (800-438-7245).

EUROSTAR: THE CHANNEL TUNNEL

Eurostar offers 12 round-trips a day through the tunnel that goes under the English Channel connecting Paris or Brussels with London. The senior fares—you're eligible if you're over 60—are about 20 percent less than the regular adult fares for first-class tickets. They are also unrestricted and refundable.
For information: Rail Europe, 800-EUROSTAR or 800-4-EURAIL (800-438-7245).

COUNTRY-BY-COUNTRY TRAVEL DEALS

AUSTRIA

In Austria, women at age 60 and men over 65 may buy half-fare passes valid on the Austrian Federal Railways and the bus system of the Federal Railways and the Postal Service (except on municipal subways, trolleys, and buses). To get the pass, you must first buy a Railway Senior Citizens ID, available at all rail stations and some major post offices in Austria as well as in Frankfurt and Munich, Germany, and in Zurich, Switzerland. You must have proof of your age (your passport) and an extra passport photo. The card is good for the calendar year and currently costs ATS 350, or about $29. It is not available in the United States but may be obtained before your trip by mail from Austria or purchased at central rail stations in Austria or Germany.

Other good deals in Austria, available to visitors of any age, are the city discount cards that may be purchased in all Austrian provinces and Vienna. The benefits of the cards vary by location, but most allow you free public transit and free or reduced admissions to sightseeing tours, museums, historic sites, and attractions, and sometimes discounts on accommodations, restaurants, and shops.

For information: Austrian National Tourist Office, PO Box 1142, New York, NY 10108-1142; 212-944-6880.

BELGIUM

The Golden Railpass for travelers over 60 gives you six free one-way train trips any time in Belgium once you've purchased it at a railroad station in that country. The cost at this writing is 1,190 Belgian francs (about $34) for second class and 1,850 francs (about $53) for first class. Your pass is also good for a companion over 55.

If you are planning a short trip, however, a better choice for you may be the Belgian Half-Fare Card. This one, available to all travelers, gives you 50 percent off the full first-class or second-class train fares for a month. Current cost is 570 francs or about $17.

For information: Belgian National Tourist Office, 780 Third Ave., New York, NY 10017; 212-758-8130.

BERMUDA

Every year Bermuda dedicates the month of February to visitors over 50. During Golden Rendezvous Month, there are daily special events, activities such as duplicate bridge and ballroom dancing and talks on the traditions, culture, history, and flora and fauna of the island, plus free bus tours to see the sights. Many hotels offer special packages and rates, and the Visitors Service Bureau in Hamilton distributes discount coupon books good at retail stores and attractions plus free ferry/bus tokens.

For information: Bermuda Department of Tourism, 310 Madison Ave., New York, NY 10017; 800-223-6106.

FRANCE

The Carte Vermeil, which allows significant discounts on train tickets on the French National Railroad (SNCF), is available to anyone over 60 and is sold in all major train stations throughout France. There are two kinds of cards, both valid for a year after they are issued. The Carte Vermeil Quatre Temps, which costs 143 francs or about $24, is good for four one-way rail trips within the year. The Carte Vermeil Plein Temps, which currently costs 279 francs or about $47, allows unlimited travel.

Both cards entitle you to a 20 or 50 percent discount, depending on when you travel, on first- or second-class tickets (except on the Paris suburban network). The 50 percent discount may be used during the *periode bleue:* Monday noon until Friday noon and Saturday noon to 3 P.M. on Sunday. The 20 percent discount applies in the *periode blanche:* Friday noon to Saturday noon and 3 P.M. Sunday until Monday noon and on certain holidays. The Carte Vermeil Plein Temps also gives you a 30 percent discount on train trips from France to more than 20 other European countries.

Don't forget to inquire about senior discounts wherever you go in France, from museums to historic sites, movies, concerts, and other cultural events.

For information: French Government Tourist Office, 444 Madison Ave., New York, NY 10022; 212-838-7800.

GREAT BRITAIN

You'll find some good bargains in the U.K. because the British favor "the very good years" and offer senior discounts and special rates on almost everything from railroads to buses, museums, day cruises, theaters, and historical sites. Wherever you go, ask if there is an OAP (Old Age Pensioners) rate. For travel information before you leave home, the British Tourist Authority is your source.

For information: British Tourist Authority, 551 Fifth Ave., Ste. 701, New York, NY 10176; 800-GO 2 BRIT (800-462-2748) or 212-986-2200.

In Britain, where virtually every town may be reached by train, it pays to consider a rail pass for your explorations, especially since travelers over 60 get discounts of 10 to 15 percent off the regular adult prices. The BritRail Senior Flexipass allows unlimited first-class travel on any 4, 8, or 15 days within a month, while the BritRail Senior Classic Pass is good on 8, 15, 22, or 30 consecutive days. The passes are not available in Great Britain but must be purchased before you leave home. They are not accepted in Ireland or on special excursion trains. With either pass, you may get on and off the trains as often as you like along the way.

By the way, here's a good deal if you are traveling with youngsters: when you use your Senior Pass (or an adult pass), one accompanying child 5 to 15 years old rides free (children under 5 are always free). Additional children up to the age of 15 travel at half-price.

Another option is the Senior Railcard, which is not available here but must be purchased at major rail stations in the U.K. Designed for residents over 60 but useful for visitors who will spend considerable time in the British Isles, it is good for a year for a flat fee of about $25. It reduces your rail fares about 30 percent.

Don't leave home without a Great British Heritage Pass, which allows unlimited free entry to almost 600 castles, abbeys, palaces, manor homes, museums, and gardens in England, Scotland, Wales, and Northern Ireland. Get it from BritRail before you leave or on arrival at the British Travel Centre.

The London Visitor Travelcard, not available in the U.K., gives you virtually unlimited travel on London Transport's underground and bus networks for 3 to 7 consecutive days as well as many trains in the London area. It includes an underground transfer from Heathrow International Airport to central London.

The Scottish Explorer Pass gives unlimited access to more than 60 of Scotland's attractions from Edinburgh Castle to the DallasDhu Distillery. It is discounted for seniors and may be obtained from Scottish Tourist Information Centers.

For information: BritRail, 1500 Broadway, New York, NY 10036; 888-BRITRAIL (888-274-8724).

If you plan to travel extensively by bus, you may want to buy a Tourist Trail Pass, good for unlimited travel on National Express and Scottish Citylink buses for varying numbers of days, before you leave this side of the Atlantic. If you're age 50 or older, you will get a substantial discount over the regular adult fare.

For information: British Travel International, PO Box 299, Elkton, VA 22827; 540-298-1395.

GREECE

Here, if you are at least 60, you may buy a rail pass, valid for a year, at any major railroad station in Greece and use it for five complimentary train trips anywhere you want to travel in the country off-season (October 1 to June 30). It is not good on the 10 days before or after Easter or Christmas. When the five free trips have been used, the pass provides you with a 50 percent discount on rail tickets. Current cost for the pass is approximately $55 for first class.

For information: Greek National Tourist Organization, 645 Fifth Ave., New York, NY 10022; 212-421-5777.

HONG KONG

Because so many visitors to Hong Kong are members of the older generation, the Hong Kong Tourist Association offers its *Mature Travellers Guide*, a booklet with useful information and practical advice, plus a list of special discounts on transportation, dining, and shopping for people over the age of 60. With it comes the Silver Plus Card. This gives you discounts, complete with instructions.

For information: Hong Kong Tourist Association, 590 Fifth Ave., New York, NY 10036-4706; 212-869-5008.

IRELAND

Many hotels in the Republic of Ireland offer senior discounts, especially off-peak, so make it a policy to inquire about them when making your reservations. In most cases, you must be 65 to qualify. Theaters (midweek), national monuments, and historic sites give you price reductions too. Always ask.

No doubt you'll be spending time in Dublin, so it would be wise to buy a Dublin Supersaver Card, which reduces the admission fees by up to 30 percent for a group of museums, castles, and attractions. Good for a year, it currently costs 16 pounds (about $25) for an adult pass, but if you are an OAP (Old Age Pensioner, for which you qualify at 60 or 65) you'll get it for 12½ pounds (about $20). It is available at Dublin Tourism Information Centres around the city.

For information: Irish Tourist Board, 345 Park Ave., New York, NY 10154; 800-223-6470 or 212-418-0800.

ITALY

The Carta d'Argenta (Silver Card), which currently costs about $20 and is valid for a year, entitles anyone over 60, tourist or resident, to a 20 percent discount on all rail travel in Italy. You buy it at railroad stations in Italy at the special windows (Biglietti Speciali) and, to get the lower fares, show it when you buy your tickets. It is not available on this side of the Atlantic. This card will obviously save you money if you plan to travel extensively in Italy, but the Flexi-Rail Pass or Italian Railcard, available to persons of any age, which may be purchased in the U.S., may prove to be a better value for shorter stays with less mileage.

Check out all of your choices before making a decision. *For information:* CIT Tours, 9501 W. Devon Ave., Rosemont, IL 60018; 800-CIT-RAIL.

LUXEMBOURG

Anybody over 65 pays half fare on trains and buses. Just show proof of age when you buy your tickets. *For information:* Luxembourg National Tourist Office, 17 Beekman Pl., New York, NY 10022; 212-935-8888.

CHECK OUT YOUR HEALTH INSURANCE

When you travel to foreign countries, remember that Medicare does not provide coverage for health-care services outside of the U.S.—except in Canada and Mexico. So if you do not have private health insurance that will pay these expenses if you incur them overseas, talk to your travel agent about purchasing temporary insurance that covers you for the length of your trip. Some policies cover trip cancellation/interruption and lost baggage as well.

NETHERLANDS

Whenever you go to museums, attractions, cultural and historic sites, or on tours in Holland, always ask if there is a senior discount because people over 65 are usually given a break on admission fees. Have your passport handy to prove your age.

If you'll be staying in the Netherlands for at least a few months, it makes sense to buy a 60+ Pass that provides you with a 40 percent discount on Dutch Railways trains, except during rush hours or on holidays. A bonus: you also get seven free travel days that may be used once every two months, with the seventh day good any time. The pass costs 99 guilders (currently about $66) at railroad stations and is valid for a year.

At age 65, you may buy a discounted *strippenkart*, giving you 15 rides on trams, buses, subways, and some trains within city limits, for about half (approximately $3 at this writing) what it costs a younger adult. It's available at post offices, train stations, and tourist offices.

In Amsterdam, consider buying an Amsterdam Culture & Leisure Pass, good for a year, at Schiphol Airport or a VVV Amsterdam Tourist Office in the city. The pass is not age-oriented, but it will give you coupons for free admission to many museums, a free canal cruise, a guided tour at a diamond-cutting house, and discounts on some restaurants and other cruises. The cost at this writing is about $19.

For information: Netherlands Board of Tourism, 225 N. Michigan Ave., Chicago IL 60601; 888-GO-HOLLAND (888-464-6552).

NEW ZEALAND

Travelers over 60 are entitled to a Golden Age discount of 30 percent off the standard adult fares on all Tranz Scenic Trains any time of year. Buy your tickets at a railroad station or a Visitor Information office in New Zealand.

For information: New Zealand Tourism Board, 501 Santa Monica Blvd., Santa Monica, CA 90401; 800-388-5494 or 310-395-7480.

PORTUGAL

If you're over 65, you can hardly go anywhere in Portugal without being offered a senior discount of 30 to 50 percent off the regular price. So make a point of asking for it when you take a train or a bus and when you go to a museum, national monument, the theater, the movies, and anyplace else that charges admission.

For information: Portuguese National Tourist Office, 590 Fifth Ave., New York, NY 10036; 212-354-4403.

SCANDINAVIAN COUNTRIES

If you are a mature traveler, Scandinavia has some good deals for you. First of all, you may travel in four Scandinavian countries—Denmark, Sweden, Norway, and Finland—less expensively than other people.

One way is to take advantage of the Scanrail 55+ Pass, which must be purchased in the U.S. before you leave home. This gives you a pass at discounted prices, if you are 55, for unlimited travel by train in all four countries. You may buy the pass for five days (to be used within 15 days), for 10 days (to be used within a month), or for a month of consecutive days, allowing you to travel wherever you like on the national rail networks. Bonuses (some of which may constitute usage of a travel day) include free passage on several water crossings, half price on several cruise lines, 25 percent discount on certain ferries, and discounts from 10 to 30 percent on hotel room rates during the months of June, July, and August.

For information: Call your travel agent or Rail Europe at 800-4-EURAIL (800-438-7245).

Another way to save when you are in the Scandinavian countries is by using the Scandinavian BonusPass. It is not age oriented but gives discounts of up to 50 percent on the room rates at over 100 first-class hotels in the summer and on weekends the rest of the year. And, in cities, consider buying city cards, which offer discounts or free entry to museums, attractions, and historic sites, and give you free public transportation. Get the cards at tourist offices, airports, or hotels. They are currently available for Copenhagen, Odense, and Aalborg in Denmark; Helsinki and Tampere in Finland; Oslo in Norway; and Stockholm, Gothenburb, and Malmo in Sweden.

For information: Scandinavian National Tourist Offices, 655 Third Ave., New York, NY 10017; 212-949-2333.

Now here are the current country-by-country savings opportunities for mature travelers:

Denmark: In this charming country, you may buy train tickets at a reduced fare—usually 50 percent of the regular adult fare—for first or second class every day of the week. Buy them at the train station and be ready to prove you are 65.

Domestic airfares are also cheaper for you at age 65 or older. SAS gives you a 10 percent discount on most fares within Denmark, and Maersk Air does the same.

Finland: The Finnish Senior Citizen Card, sold for about $9 at railroad or bus stations, entitles you at age 65 to half fare on trains and 30 percent off on bus trips that are at least 80 kilometers one way. You'll also get a great discount—70 percent—on Finnair's domestic flights just for being over 65. You must pay for your tickets within three days of booking your flight.

Norway: In Norway you must pay only half price for a train ticket, first or second class, any time, any place, and the same applies to bus fares. For this break, however, you or your spouse traveling together must be at least 67 and, if asked by the ticket agent or driver, prove it with a proper ID. Also at 67 you become eligible for a discount on Norwegian Coastal Voyages (except from June 1 to July 15) and, at 60, half price on Color Line cruises to England and the Continent (see Chapter 5). And there's more: SAS offers passengers over 65 a 50 percent discount on all flights within Norway. This discounted fare may be purchased only in Norway.

Sweden: If you buy the inexpensive Reslust Card in Sweden, you will pay 25 percent less than younger adults do on all train journeys over 50 miles on Tuesdays, Wednesdays, Thursdays, and Saturdays. And you may also take advantage of discounts in dining cars, special summer rates, and more. The card, which costs everyone else about $18, costs you at 65 and over only about $7.

On flights within Sweden, SAS gives passengers 65 and over special senior fares, the amounts depending on the route. Be sure to ask about them.

SWITZERLAND

The Swiss Hotel Association will provide, for the asking, a list of over 450 hotels that participate in the Season for Seniors, giving reduced rates to women over 62 and men over 65 (if you are a couple, only one of you must be the required minimum age). The only catch is that in most cases the lower rates do not apply during peak travel periods, including the summer months.

The Swiss Museum Passport, good for a month, gives you admission to about 180 museums for $25 if you are a woman over 62 or a man over 65. That's $5 less than it costs a younger adult. It is available at participating museums, tourist offices, and train stations in Switzerland.

For information: Switzerland Tourism, 608 Fifth Ave., New York, NY 10020; 212-757-5944.

5

Trips and Tours for the Mature Traveler

Many enterprising organizations, tour operators, and travel agencies now cater only to the mature traveler. They choose destinations sure to appeal to those who have already seen much of the world, arrange trips that are leisurely and unhassled, give you congenial contemporaries to travel with and group hosts to smooth the way, and provide many special services you never got before. They also give you a choice between strenuous action-filled tours and those that are more relaxed. In fact, most of the agencies offer so many choices that the major problem becomes making a decision about where to go.

Options range from cruises in the Caribbean or the Greek Isles to grand tours of the Orient, sight-seeing excursions in the United States, trips to the Canadian Rockies, theater tours of London, African safaris, and snorkeling vacations on the Great Barrier Reef off Australia. There's just no place in the world where over-50s won't go.

Among the newer and most popular trends are apartment/hotel complexes in American and European resort areas, as well as apartments in major cities. Here you can stay put for as long as you like, using the apartment or hotel as a home base for short-range roaming and exploring with the guidance of on-site hosts.

To qualify for some of the trips, one member of the party must meet the minimum age requirement, while the others may be younger.

TRIPS FOR THE MATURE TRAVELER

AFC TOURS

Specializing in escorted tours designed for mature travelers, AFC schedules trips to all the most popular destinations in the U.S. and Canada and some in other countries. Not only that, but if you live in southern California, where AFC is based, you will be transported between your home and the airport. Domestic tours take you to such places as the national parks, Washington, D.C., Branson, Nashville, New York City, Savannah, and New Orleans. International adventures cover all of Europe. Other choices: cruises, steamboating, train tours, holiday tours, and grandparent trips. In other words, almost anything you want. Special for singles: If you sign up four months in advance and a roommate cannot be found to share your room, you need not pay a single supplement.

For information: AFC Tours, 11772 Sorrento Valley Rd., San Diego, CA 92121; 800-369-3693 or 619-481-8188.

BACK-ROADS TOURING CO.

Designed especially for adults over 50, the tours planned by Back-Roads Touring Co. take groups of no more than 12 participants on explorations of England, Scotland, Wales, Ireland, or France, along the back roads to out-of-the-way places. You'll travel by minivan with a knowledgeable local guide for one or two weeks, lodge in historic houses, inns, or bed and breakfasts, and won't spend a fortune. These are leisurely tours with plenty of time to explore. You'll stay several nights in the same location, spend time with local residents. You may even help plan the itinerary. Add-on stays in London are available, too, and so are four-day "country breaks" and day trips out of London. What's more, if you mention this book, you will get a discount.

For information: Back-Roads Touring Co., British Network Ltd., 594 Valley Rd., Upper Montclair, NJ 07043; 800-274-8583 or 201-744-5215. In Canada, contact Golden Escapes, 75 The Donway West, Ste. 710, Don Mills, ON M3C 2E9; 800-668-9125 or 416-447-7683.

CIE TOURS INTERNATIONAL

An agency whose trips go only to Ireland, Scotland, Wales, and England, CIE offers motorcoach tours and fly/drive vacations, many of which come with a 55 and Smiling Discount. This means that on certain departure dates you get $55 per person off the cost of the trip if you are 55 or older. If you want to organize your own group of travelers, CIE will arrange a coach tour for you.

For information: CIE Tours International, 100 Hanover Ave., Cedar Knolls, NJ 07927; 800 CIE-TOUR (800-243-8687) or 973-292-3438.

KEEP POSTED ON PERKS

Here's a newsletter with an attitude! *The Over-50 Thrifty Traveler* celebrates the positive side of getting older, keeps track of the perks, aims to save you money, and insists that being over 50 can be lots of fun. For "baby boomers and young-thinking seniors of all ages," the eight-page monthly newsletter, full of money-saving suggestions and useful advice, costs $29 a year for a subscription.

For information: The Over-50 Thrifty Traveler, PO Box 8168, Clearwater, FL 33758; 800-532-5731 or 813-447-4731.

COLLETTE TOURS

The worry-free vacations for the mature population from Collette Tours, an escorted-tour operator for the last 80 years, include over 100 itineraries in more than 50 countries from South America to Asia, Europe, Africa, and our own continent. It even offers grand tours of South America or East Asia. Its trips move at a relaxed pace, put you up in good hotels, and provide experienced tour guides to see that everything goes well. In such places as Costa Rica, Denmark, Scotland, Portugal, Spain, Israel, and Austria, the agency's "Hub and Spoke" programs feature several days in one place so you don't have to keep packing and unpacking your bags. Meanwhile, day excursions take you to see the sights.

For information: Collette Tours, 162 Middle St., Pawtucket, RI 02860; 800-832-4656.

CORLISS TOURS

The Stay-Put Tours by Corliss are planned with older travelers in mind—you fly to your destination, check into your hotel, hang up your clothes, and stay put, never packing your bags again until it's time to go home. Meanwhile, you go on local tours and day trips to interesting places nearby. Each tour carries along a tour director who makes all the arrangements and shepherds the group around. Plenty of time, too, to relax and explore on your own. Destinations include Atlanta, Orlando, Washington, D.C., New York, Philadelphia, San Antonio, Seattle, Denver, Colorado Springs, Nashville, New Orleans, Montreal, Plymouth, Chicago, Toronto, Ottawa, Calgary, and Vancouver. Each tour lasts a week, but you may link two or more trips as you like. This agency also organizes tours, many of them Stay-Puts, over the Thanksgiving and Christmas holidays, taking you to resorts, festivals, and popular vacation destinations such as Washington, D.C., Williamsburg, New Orleans, Branson, Myrtle Beach, and Scottsdale.

For information: Corliss Tours, 436 W. Foothill Blvd., Monrovia, CA 91016; 800-456-5717.

DELTA QUEEN STEAMSHIP CO.

Steamboating, always popular among mature travelers, is the specialty of this company, whose steam-powered overnight paddle wheelers ply the Mississippi River and other inland waterways on 2- to 14-night cruises. Among other offerings are big band cruises, a Dixie fest, voyages for Civil War buffs with lectures by historians and visits to battle sites, 1950s dance tours, cruises that celebrate Elvis Presley or Mark Twain, and "Year That Was" trips celebrating 1946, 1948, or 1950.

For information: Delta Queen Steamship Co., 30 Robin Street Wharf, New Orleans, LA 70130-1890; 800-543-1949.

ELDERTREKS

If you insist on viewing the world through bus windows or on sleeping in five-star hotels, stop reading now, because on ElderTreks' trips you'll be doing a lot of walking and maybe you'll sleep in a tribal village. ElderTreks is a program of adventure tours for travelers 50 and over (and companions of any age) who are in reasonably good physical condition, capable of walking at a comfortable pace in tropical conditions. Featuring exotic adventures to relatively remote places in the world, it stresses cultural interaction, physical activity, and nature exploration. However, trekking routes are chosen with older hikers in mind and groups are limited to 15. Trekking portions of the trips are optional and you may choose to substitute a guesthouse-based itinerary.

Accommodations for the city portions of the tours are in clean, comfortable tourist-class hotels and guesthouses chosen for charm and location. Accommodations on the adventure portions may be on the floor of a nomadic tent or under a canopy of trees in the jungle, but you can always count on having an air mattress to sleep on. Guides, cooks, and porters are part of the package. Destinations include Thailand, Borneo, Vietnam, Laos, Sumatra, Java, Bali, China, Tibet, Nepal, India, Turkey, Ecuador and the Galapagos Islands, Costa Rica, Bolivia, Peru, Madagasgar, Morocco, Yemen, Iceland, New Zealand, and Belize.
For information: ElderTreks, 597 Markham St., Toronto, ON M6G 2L7; 800-741-7956 or 416-588-5000.

FANCY-FREE HOLIDAYS

Geared for senior travelers, this agency's domestic escorted motorcoach tours include all of the usual favorite destinations such as Branson, New England, Alaska, Williamsburg, Asheville, New Orleans, and Washington, D.C. Its fully escorted overseas tours by air, motorcoach, or cruise ship include Ireland, Kenya, Poland, Italy, Germany, South America, and the Baltic Sea. A special feature: most domestic motorcoach tours are fully refundable right up to the day of departure.

For information: Fancy-Free Holidays, 236 S. Washington, Naperville, IL 60540; 800-421-3330 or 630-778-7010.

SAMPLING RETIREMENT COMMUNITIES

If you are searching for the perfect place to retire but don't know where to start, consider taking an "inspection trip" offered by **Retirement Consultants International** (RCI) to look over the possibilities. As your destination, choose among many popular areas in Florida, the Carolinas, Arizona, California, or Nevada. With a basic fly-drive package, you get a moderately priced package that includes air, hotel accommodations for six or seven nights, and a car rental—plus a day-by-day itinerary, maps and directions, and a destination profile describing geographic features, climate and weather, demographics, tax information, cost-of-living data, and a list of cultural, religious, and medical facilities.

You make the trip on your own at your own pace and visit as many retirement villages within range as you wish. Drive-yourself trips that include hotel accommodations and a destination kit are also available.

For information: RCI, 50 E. Palisade Ave., Englewood, NJ 07631; 800-662-4667 or 201-816-1390.

GALAXY TOURS

Galaxy Tours takes former American GIs and their families on nostalgic journeys to visit the places where they once served overseas. The most popular tour returns to the scenes of the Battle of the Bulge of World War II. Others retrace the route of the American forces into Normandy on D-Day or take you to Germany if you were stationed there after the war. Veterans of the Korean or Vietnam Wars are also offered group tours to revisit the lands they once knew so well.

For information: Galaxy Tours, PO Box 234, Wayne, PA 19087-0234; 800-523-7287 or 610-964-8010.

GO AHEAD VACATIONS

Go Ahead Vacations, a division of EF Education, a company that has specialized for over 30 years in intercultural exchange and educational travel, plans a wide array of holidays exclusively for the mature crowd. Its European Leisure Program, designed for independent people who prefer not to be part of a group tour, takes you to popular cities on the Continent. Here you stay in a hotel, breakfast included, and manage your own holiday with the help of an on-site coordinator. If instead you choose an all-inclusive program, you will stay for a week or more in a resort hotel in such places as the Canary Islands, Crete, or Spain's Costa del Sol, where meals and sight-seeing are included. The third option from Go Ahead includes a wide range of traditional escorted motorcoach tours and cruises to just about anywhere you've ever wanted to go.

If you request a roommate, you'll get one or have your single supplement reduced by half.

For information: Go Ahead Vacations, EF Center Boston, 1 Education St., Cambridge MA 02141; 800-242-4686.

GOLDEN AGE FESTIVAL TRAVEL

Another agency that caters to the mature crowd, this one offers escorted tours to everywhere from Wildwood (New Jersey), Myrtle Beach, Nashville, Maine, and New York to the national parks, Las Vegas, Europe, Greece, and Hawaii. Plus plenty of cruises. All packages are escorted and include accommodations, meals, and just about everything else.

In addition, Golden Age Festival offers an innovation—drive-to tours for individual travelers, allowing them to take advantage of group discounts that make the trips remarkably inexpensive. On these, all on the East Coast, you drive yourself to your destination—for example, Wildwood, Ocean City, Myrtle Beach, Newport and Mystic Seaport, Hilton Head, Williamsburg—and join others traveling on their own for meals, entertainment, and tours.

For information: Golden Age Festival Travel, 5501 New Jersey Ave., Wildwood Crest, NJ 08260; 800-257-8920 or 609-522-6316.

GOLDEN AGE TRAVELLERS

This over-50 club's specialty is discounted cruises on major cruise lines everywhere in the world, but it offers land tours from well-known tour operators as well. When you join the club ($10 or $15 per couple a year), you receive a quarterly newsletter with listings of upcoming sailings. Other inducements are tour escorts and bonus points. Single travelers may choose to be enrolled in the Roommates

Wanted list to help them find companions to share cabins and costs. For members in the San Francisco and Sacramento areas, there are one-day excursions and meetings where you may meet fellow travelers.

Especially intriguing to mature travelers are this agency's long-stay trips. On these, you stay put—for example, in Spain, Portugal, Guatemala, Australia, Costa Rica, or Argentina—at the same hotel for two or three weeks, and, if you wish, take short side trips. The packages include air, hotel, and sometimes meals.

For information: Golden Age Travellers, Pier 27, the Embarcadero, San Francisco, CA 94111; 800-258-8880 or 415-563-2361.

GOLDEN ESCAPES

Golden Escapes for the 50-Plus Traveller is a Canadian agency that offers all-inclusive escorted tours in Canada, the U.S., and Europe as well as three-week tours of such exotic places as Greece, Egypt, Cyprus, Turkey, Tunisia, and South Africa. It also has long-stay programs where you lodge in an apartment or a hotel in a resort area—perhaps Portugal's Algarve, Newport Beach, Palm Springs, or the island of Crete—and take excursions by day, highlighted by parties, happy hours, entertainment, and other activities.

In addition, Golden Escapes is the representative in Canada for Back-Roads Touring Co., which takes you on minicoach tours of England, France, Scotland, or Ireland. Other sight-seeing adventures for over-50s include trips to popular U.S. destinations, including Washington, D.C., Myrtle Beach, Savannah, and Cape Cod.

For information: Golden Escapes, 75 The Donway West, Ste. 710, Don Mills, ON M3C 2E9; 800-668-9125 or 416-447-7683.

GRAND CIRCLE TRAVEL

Grand Circle caters to people over 50 and plans all of its trips exclusively for them. The first U.S. company to market senior travel, it specializes in Live Abroad Extended Stay Vacations. Sign up and you will live in an apartment, villa, or house in a foreign country for anywhere from 2 to 26 weeks at a moderate cost. At the moment, you may choose to live in Turkey, Italy, Greece, Spain, Portugal, Majorca, Malta, Central Europe, or Mexico. You may decide to be on your own during your stay or to use the services of the on-site program director who is always available to help you plan your days.

Traditional escorted tours are on the menu, too, taking you to destinations all over the world on international or domestic land trips as well as sea cruises and river cruises on small chartered boats on the Danube, Rhine, Yangtze, and Nile Rivers. Grand Circle's Discovery Series is another option, offering educational/travel trips to interesting foreign destinations where you become immersed in the local culture, history, art, environment, and politics. You'll visit local families, take language lessons, learn to cook regional foods, attend lectures, and learn all about the country you are visiting.

Single travelers with GCT pay only half of the single supplements on most trips when they have requested a travel roommate and none is available. And on a few Live

Abroad departure dates, they pay no supplements at all.

GCT donates about half a million dollars a year to a foundation that funds humanitarian and environmental projects around the world. It is also associated with Overseas Adventure Travel. See Chapter 3.

For information: Grand Circle Travel, 347 Congress St., Boston, MA 02210; 800-248-3737 or 617-350-7500. Ask for the free booklet *101 Tips for Mature Travelers*.

IDYLL, LTD.

The "untours" of Europe planned by Idyll are a cross between independent travel and organized group tours. They fly you to the country of your choice; escort you to your own apartment, chalet, or farmhouse; provide you with local escorts and guides, maps, rail passes, and itineraries and a chance to live like the local people for two or four weeks. Round-trip air and ground transportation are included.

For information: Idyll, Ltd., PO Box 405, Media, PA 19063; 610-565-5242.

MAYFLOWER TOURS

Most of Mayflower's travelers are "55 or better," so the pace of its tours is leisurely and rest stops are scheduled every couple of hours. You travel by motorcoach, stay in good hotels or motels, and eat many of your meals together. All trips are fully escorted by tour directors who make sure all goes well. If you are a single traveler and request a roommate at least 30 days before departure, you'll get a roommate or a room to yourself at the regular double rate. Tours go almost everywhere in the United States and Canada, including national parks of the Southwest, the Canadian Rockies and Pacific Northwest, French Canada, Branson and the Ozarks, New England and Cape Cod, Hawaii, and New York. Cruises take you to the Caribbean, the Panama Canal, Alaska, Hawaii, or the New England coast.

For information: Mayflower Tours, 1225 Warren Ave., Downers Grove, IL 60515; 800-323-7604 or 630-960-3430.

MID-LIFE ADVENTURES

If you're hankering for a bit of adventure and want to travel with a small companionable group of people who are at least 35 years old, consider the tours of New Zealand offered by Mid-Life Adventures. Scheduled for departures during New Zealand's summer—October through mid-April—you'll have moderately paced outdoor experiences as you travel all over the North or South Islands—or both—seeing the sights and visiting five national and two maritime parks. Owned by "a mature couple" and led by "mature" guides, this agency will take you sailing, whitewater rafting, sea kayaking, cave rafting, sight-seeing, hiking, and on glacier walks, bush walks, and scenic flights, for which you need no previous experience but must be in good physical shape.

For information: Mid-Life Adventures, 11901 Santa Monica Blvd., West Los Angeles, CA 90025; 800-528-6129 or 310-998-5880.

PLEASANT HAWAIIAN HOLIDAYS

Pleasant's Makua Club Holidays are special packages for vacationers over the age of 55, at a choice of more than 45 hotels and condos on four Hawaiian islands. There's nothing to join and no dues to pay, and only one person per room needs to be the right age. You get complimentary room upgrades, car-rental upgrades, and a $25 certificate per room to use when you buy an optional event, activity, or excursion. Pleasant also runs many specials, so check them out to find the best deal for you.

For information: Pleasant Hawaiian Holidays, 2404 Townsgate Rd., Westlake, CA 91361; 800-2-HAWAII (800-242-9244).

RFD TOURS

Created many years ago to arrange visits between American and foreign farmers, and then to organize flower and garden tours, RFD Travel now plans a wide range of U.S. and international tours and cruises every year specifically for mature travelers. All hosted, the trips stress cultural heritage events, personal encounters with local residents, knowledgeable tour managers, and an easy pace.

For information: RFD Tours, 1225 Warren Ave., Downers Grove, IL 60515; 800-365-5359 or 630-960-3974.

SAGA HOLIDAYS

Saga plans trips exclusively for travelers over 50 and their younger traveling companions. It offers an astonishing variety of vacations, from fully escorted, all-inclusive tours of any place you've ever wanted to visit to cruises and safaris, educational travel, walking tours, and winter resort stays. It also offers grand tours of Europe, holidays in Turkey or Greece, nature tours of Borneo, river cruises down the Danube River or the Yangtze River in China.

All-inclusive resort holidays are designed to let you live a while in one place—in Portugal, Spain, Sicily, Costa Rica, Ecuador, Nicaragua, Turkey, or Greece—where you settle into your hotel for a relaxing stay-put vacation that includes entertainment, activities, and excursions.

In 1996, Saga introduced the *Saga Rose*, its own cruise ship, and a variety of voyages in European waters. The only cruise ship that caters exclusively to over-50s, its itineraries and amenities are tailored for mature customers.

Associated with Saga, too, are two educational travel programs. Smithsonian Odyssey Tours, in partnership with the famed Smithsonian Institution, gives you a wide choice of learning adventures guided by experts in their fields. Among recent choices: Egypt's ancient temples, the Mayan culture, the mysteries of Machu Picchu, Moorish castles in Spain and Portugal, imperial Russian waterways, and the cultural treasures of Ireland.

The Road Scholar program's travel-study itineraries each have a special theme, such as French impressionism, British mystery novels, the geology of Iceland, the paintings and palaces of St. Petersburg, and Dutch and Flemish art, again with lectures by experts from academic or cultural institutions.

For information: Saga Holidays, 222 Berkeley St., Boston, MA 02116; 800-343-0273. Smithsonian Odysseys: 800-258-5885. Road Scholar programs: 800-621-2151. *Saga Rose*: 800-952-9590.

SCI/NATIONAL RETIREES OF AMERICA

This agency, which began decades ago with trips to the Catskills resorts, now offers a long list of escorted group tours for seniors that range from 1-day outings to 45-day world cruises. The land tours—5-day jaunts by air to Las Vegas are its specialty—depart midweek, transport you by motorcoach, and take you to such places as New Orleans, Quebec, Niagara Falls, the Poconos, Orlando, Nashville, or New York.

For information: SCI/National Retirees of America, 1188 Grand Ave., Baldwin, NY 11510; 800-698-1101 or 516-485-3200.

MEXICAN PREVIEW

A California travel company, **Barvi Tours**, conducts a weekly five-night trip to Guadalajara, a popular retirement city in Mexico, for those who are contemplating retirement there. Here you tour the residential areas of Chapala and Ajijic on the shore of the largest lake in Mexico, explore the area, talk to residents, and learn from experts about cultural differences, personal finances, medical services, housing, immigration laws, cost of living, and shopping.

For information: Barvi Tours, 11658 Gateway Blvd., Los Angeles, CA 90064; 800-824-7102 or 310-474-4041.

SENIORITY ADVENTURES

These trips, all originating from Houston, Texas, take groups of seniors on motorcoach tours and cruises to some of their favorite destinations in the U.S., such as Branson, Washington, D.C., southern California, Yellowstone, New England, and Alaska. One of Seniority's specialties is short trips close to home in the vast state of Texas: Big Bend country, Aransas National Wildlife Refuge to spot whooping cranes, and Tyler to see the roses. It also offers a few adventures to foreign lands.

For information: Seniority Adventures, PO Box 709, Sugar Land, TX 77487; 281-491-6565.

TRAFALGAR TOURS

After 50 years of taking Americans on tours of Europe, Trafalgar has now added a first-class tour program in the U.S. and Canada with more than a dozen regional itineraries. Catering to older travelers who want to see the sights without worrying about logistics and details, these escorted motorcoach tours include luxury coaches, first-class hotels or lodges, guided sight-seeing, gratuities, and most meals. Trafalgar also continues its overseas tours, both first-class and budget, to Europe, Britain, and South Africa. Traveling alone? You'll be matched with an appropriate roommate.

For information: Trafalgar Tours USA, 11 East 16 St., New York, NY 10010-1402; 800-854-0103 or 212-725-7776.

VALUE WORLD TOURS

An agency that specializes in trips to central and eastern Europe, Value World Tours takes 10 to 20 percent off the cost of some of its river cruises and escorted tours during off-peak seasons for travelers over the age of 50. River cruises include trips on inland waterways in Russia, Ukraine, central Europe, and China, while the hosted or escorted motorcoach tours go to many destinations in eastern Europe such as Latvia, Estonia, Lithuania, Poland, Hungary, and Russia.

For information: Value World Tours, 17220 Newhope St., Fountain Valley, CA 92708; 800-795-1633 or 714-556-8258.

VANTAGE DELUXE WORLD TRAVEL

Vantage features upscale tours for mature travelers and since 1983 has escorted more than a quarter of a million over-50 tourists around the world on land tours and cruises. Accommodations are always deluxe and explorations are leisurely and relaxed, so there is plenty of time to savor the sights. All trips are led by tour directors who see to it that everything—from ticketing and baggage handling to check-ins, meals, and tips—is taken care of for you. Among Vantage's most popular tours are a Danube River cruise, a trip through the Panama Canal, a visit to China and the Yangtze River, and an exploration of Ireland or the countries of Eastern Europe. Plus longer, more exotic tours such as a 33-day tour around the world.

If you are traveling alone and want a roommate, a compatible companion will be found or half the single supplement on land programs will be waived.

For information: Vantage Deluxe World Travel, 111 Cypress St., Brookline, MA 02146; 800-784-0935. Ask for the free booklets *99 Travel Tips for Mature Travellers* and *Health Guide for Older Travellers.*

VISTA TOURS

Another agency providing escorted tours almost exclusively for the mature set, Vista Tours plans leisurely trips with plenty of stops and ample time to enjoy the points of interest and relax too. You travel on comfortable motorcoaches with escorts who deal with the reservations, transfers, luggage, meal arrangements, and all other potentially problematic situations. Destinations, although mainly in the U.S., also include Canada, France, the Far East, Australia, and New Zealand. A highlight every year is a five-day trip over the New Year's holiday to California for the Pasadena Rose Parade and a New Year's Eve party with a big band and a celebrity show. If you're a woman who doesn't have a dancing partner or wants a better one, you may take your turn whirling around the floor with one of the gentleman hosts who accompany the group.

For information: Vista Tours, 1923 N. Carson St., Ste. 105, Carson City, NV 89701; 800-647-0800.

CRUISING THE HIGH SEAS

Cruises have always appealed to the mature crowd. In fact, most sailings abound with people who are at least several decades out of college. So you are sure to find suitable companionship. However, never sign up for a vacation at sea without shopping around for a discount because you rarely have to pay the advertised rate. Work with your own travel agent or call a discount cruise agency such as The Cruise Line (800-777-0707) or World Wide Cruises (800-882-9000) to search out the best deals available when and where you want to travel.

In the meantime, for starters, here are some senior specials designed especially for you.

BALLROOM DANCERS WITHOUT PARTNERS

Are you a single person over 50 who loves to dance? Look into the many cruises scheduled every year by this agency that caters to solo travelers who love dancing more than anything. Both beginning and accomplished dancers get a chance to learn new steps during the day, go to cocktail parties with dancing before dinner, and dance again after the evening's entertainment. One male host, an excellent dancer, goes along for every five passengers in the group. BDWP will arrange cabin shares so you may avoid the single surcharge. Both big bands and Latin rhythms are featured, and itineraries take you everywhere from the Caribbean to Alaska.

For information: Ballroom Dancers Without Partners, 1449 NW 15th St., Miami, FL 33125; 800-778-7953 or 561-361-9384.

BERGEN LINE

The cruises in Scandinavia of Color Line and Norwegian Coastal Voyages, both represented in the U.S. by Bergen Line, offer special discounts to older travelers.

Color Line, Norway's largest cruise passenger company that cruises the North Sea and travels to England and the Continent, gives travelers over 60 and a companion half-price fares on many of its trips.

And Norwegian Coastal Voyages, with ships that take you along Norway's spectacular coast from Bergen to Kirkenes, north of the Arctic Circle, gives a break to passengers over the age of 67. It takes about $200 per person off the 12-day 2,500-mile round-trip fares and about $100 per person off the 6- or 7-day one-way fares (except from June 1 to July 15).

For information: Bergen Line, 800-323-7436 or 212-319-1300.

CARNIVAL CRUISE LINES

If you belong to AARP, you are entitled to savings on staterooms on many of Carnival's cruises. You'll save $200 per stateroom in categories 6 through 12 on seven-day voyages or $50 on shorter cruises to the Bahamas, the Caribbean, Hawaii, Mexico, and Alaska. Your membership number must be provided when your trip is booked.

For information: Carnival Cruise Lines, 800-CARNIVAL (800-227-6482). Or AARP, 800-887-3529.

HOLLAND AMERICA LINE

If you are a member of AARP and book an outside stateroom on a Holland America cruise or Alaska cruise tour of seven days or longer, you can save $100 per stateroom. On shorter cruises, the savings is $50 per stateroom. To get the discounts, your membership number must be provided when your trip is booked.

For information: Holland America Line, 800-887-3529.

ROYAL CARIBBEAN INTERNATIONAL

Check with your travel agent to find out when this popular cruise line will be offering one of its special deals for seniors, because the cost on these sailings, many of them scheduled in the off-peak seasons, is always less than the lowest standard discounted rates. If one passenger in your cabin is over the age of 55 and books passage early, your entire party gets the same deal. RCI's brochure indicates the activity level and amount of walking on each shore excursion.

For information: Royal Caribbean International, 800 327-6700.

ROYAL HAWAIIAN CRUISES

These day trips—some of them luncheon or dinner cruises—take you along exclusive routes on small ships or adventure rafts for snorkeling, exploring, whale watching, and sight-seeing in the Hawaiian Islands. You are entitled to a 15 percent discount on all cruises when you have reached the age of 65, so be sure to ask for it when you make your reservations.

For information: Royal Hawaiian Cruises, 800-852-4183.

MERRY WIDOWS DANCE CRUISES

Designed for solo women from 50 to 90 who love to dance but don't have partners, the **Merry Widows Dance Tours** runs many cruises every year to such places as the Caribbean, Southeast Asia, Alaska, Greece and the Mediterranean, and the Panama Canal. The trips range from 7 days to 18. Sponsored by the AAA Auto Club South, the cruises take along their own gentleman hosts, one professional dancer for every five women. Each woman receives a dance card that rotates her partners every night throughout the cruise, whether she's a beginner or a polished dancer. The men are also rotated at the dinner tables so everyone gets the pleasure of their company. You don't have to be a widow and you don't even have to know the cha-cha or the macarena to enjoy these trips.

Merry Widows also operates tours to major resorts, in such settings as the Cloister in Georgia's Sea Islands and Sedona Spa in Arizona. Out-of-the-country resort destinations include European capitals, the Greek Isles and Turkey, Tahiti, Hawaii, and the Caribbean.

For information: Call your travel agent or contact Merry Widows Dance Tours, 1515 N. Westshore Blvd., Tampa, FL 33607; 800-374-2689.

SAGA ROSE

The voyages of Saga Holidays' new cruise ship, the 580-passenger *Saga Rose* (formerly Cunard's *Sagafjord*), cater exclusively to over-50 travelers. Based in England, the ship sails European waters and has inaugurated a cruise that takes 97 days to sail around the world.

For information: Saga Holidays, 800-952-9590.

WORLD EXPLORER CRUISES

When its ship, the *S.S. Universe Explorer*, is not serving as a floating university campus (see Chapter 16), it cruises to Alaska, the Caribbean, and Central and South America. Members of AARP get discounts of 20 percent on brochure rates on all voyages in cabin categories 3 through 7. Single travelers pay a supplement of only 125 percent in the same cabin categories. And friends and family cruise free in third or fourth berth in categories 3 through 5. You or your travel agent must mention the offer and provide your membership number when booking a cruise.

For information: World Explorer Cruises, 800-854-3835.

CRUISE ESCORTS WANTED

Because single men of a certain age are scarce among the traveling population, especially on board ship, a growing number of cruise lines offer free or inexpensive travel to carefully chosen unattached men over 45 —in some cases, over 65—with excellent social and dancing skills. These gentlemen hosts serve as dancing or dining partners, make a fourth for bridge, act as escorts for shore trips, and socialize without favoritism—with the single women on board.

There are stringent screening procedures and many more applicants than positions, so don't be surprised if you are not encouraged to apply. Hosts must provide their own wardrobes and sometimes their own airfare as well as a fee to the placement agency for every week at sea.

American Hawaii Cruises takes two dancing hosts on its Big Band cruises. On this cruise line that provides weekly seven-day cruises to four islands in Hawaii, the hosts, who are knowledgeable about the islands, mingle with the guests and help the single passengers enjoy their voyages and shore excursions.

For information: American Hawaii Cruises, Entertainment Dept., 2100 N. Nimitz Hwy., Honolulu, HI 96819.

Commodore Cruise Line's ship, *Enchanted Isle*, which sails every Saturday from the Port of New Orleans to Montego Bay in Jamaica, Grand Cayman, and Cozumel and Playa del Carmen in Mexico, takes at least two male dance hosts on every cruise. Single, over-50, retired or semi-retired businessmen, their job is to attend all dance lessons and to dance with passengers to live music each night of the seven-night voyage.

For information: Karp Enterprises, 1999 University Drive, Coral Springs, FL 33071; 954-341-9400.

Crystal Cruises, whose worldwide cruises carry three or four hosts per trip, look for personable social hosts over the age of 65 who are great dancers and enjoy keeping older single women passengers entertained both on board and ashore.

For information: Entertainment Dept., Crystal Cruises, 2121 Avenue of the Stars, Los Angeles, CA 90067.

Cunard Line's cruises aboard *Queen Elizabeth 2*, the *Vistafjord*, and the *Royal Viking Sun* carry along four to ten friendly gentleman hosts between the ages of 45 and 70. Their job is

not only to whirl around the dance floor with women who need partners but to act as friendly diplomats who help passengers get to know one another. A knowledge of foreign languages is a plus.
For information: Working Vacation, 610 Pine Grove Ct., New Lenox, IL 60451; 815-485-8307.

The Delta Queen Steamship Co., which makes about 50 cruises a year up and down the Mississippi River, taking you back in time aboard huge paddle wheelers, employs mature and responsible male hosts, assigning two to each trip on the *Mississippi Queen* and four to each Big Band cruise. Their job is to dance with the single women aboard, organize activities, and help everyone enjoy the voyage.
For information: Working Vacation, 610 Pine Grove Ct., New Lenox, IL 60451; 815-485-8307.

Holland America Line recruits retired professionals with good social skills to act as hosts on its long cruises and Big Band Sailings. Usually four to six hosts go along on each trip.
For information: Working Vacation, 610 Pine Grove Ct., New Lenox, IL 60451; 815-485-8307.

Merry Widows Dance Cruises offers many cruises and land tours for single, widowed, or divorced women who were born to dance. Accompanying them are gentleman hosts (one for every five women) to serve as dance partners.
For information: Merry Widows Dance Tours, 1515 N. Westshore Blvd., Tampa, FL 33607; 800-374-2689.

Orient Lines, whose ship, the *Marco Polo*, sails to New Zealand and Australia, the Far East, Africa, India, and the Mediterranean, takes three or four male hosts along on most cruises to act as dance and dinner partners for the women aboard who don't have dancing partners.

For information: Working Vacation, 610 Pine Grove Ct., New Lenox, IL 60451; 815-485-8307.

Regal Cruises, whose ship the *Regal Empress* sails all around the coast of South America on 53-night cruises departing spring and fall, assigns three gentleman hosts to socialize with the guests.
For information: Working Vacation, 610 Pine Grove Ct., New Lenox, IL 60451; 815-485-8307.

Royal Cruise Line has a roster of screened 50-plus men to act as unofficial hosts on its cruise ships. With four to eight hosts aboard each ship, these congenial fellows spend their evenings whirling around the dance floor, doing their best to see that solo women travelers have a good time.
For information: Host Program, Royal Cruise Line, 1 Maritime Plaza, Ste. 1400, San Francisco, CA 94111.

Royal Olympic Cruises takes two professional hosts on all of its cruises of seven days or longer. Their assignment is to dance with the women who love to dance but haven't brought partners with them.
For information: Cruise Crafts International; 407-365-4426.

Silverseas Cruises has introduced gentleman hosts aboard the sister ships *Silver Cloud* and *Silver Wind*. The hosts' job is to dance, mingle, and mix, making sure all guests have an enjoyable voyage.
For information: Working Vacation, 610 Pine Grove Ct., New Lenox, IL 60451; 815-485-8307.

World Explorer Cruises: The *Universe Explorer*, whose winter ports are in Alaska and summer ports in the Caribbean and Central America, takes a couple of hosts along on all sailings.
For information: Working Vacation, 610 Pine Grove Ct., New Lenox, IL 60451; 815-485-8307.

6

Singles on the Road

More and more people of all ages book trips today unaccompanied and, to encourage and accommodate them, there are increasing numbers of tours planned exclusively for single travelers. Several major tour companies catering to mature travelers now schedule singles-only departures on which you mingle with others on their own, and many have reduced or even dropped the single-supplement charge on at least some of their tours so you may not have to pay for the privilege of a single room.

If, however, you are single, single again, or have a spouse who isn't the traveling kind and don't want to go places by yourself even in a group, consider joining a club that will help match you up with a fellow traveler who is also looking for a compatible person with whom to share adventures, a room, and expenses. Traveling with another person is usually more enjoyable and certainly less expensive than going alone because you share double accommodations, thereby avoiding the usual single supplement, which can be substantial.

MATCHMAKERS

TRAVEL COMPANION EXCHANGE

TCE specializes in helping single travelers find compatible travel partners. Managed by travel expert Jens Jurgen, Travel Companion Exchange is the largest, most enduring, and most successful matchmaking service. In fact, it has recently absorbed several other travel-partner services, including Golden Companions.

Members of TCE receive bulky bimonthly newsletters packed with travel tips and helpful advice plus long listings of people (TCE now has close to 3,000 active members) who are seeking new friends and/or travel partners of the same or opposite sex. For more information about those who seem to be good possibilities, you send for Profile Pages about them (meanwhile, others send for yours) so you may judge their suitability for yourself and then do your own matchmaking. Jurgen suggests you talk by telephone, correspond, meet, and, even better, take a short trip together before setting out on a major adventure.

You may join TCE at an introductory fee of $99 for eight months, using a credit card if you wish. By the way, you don't have to join to subscribe to the *TCE Newsletter* (without the listings) for $48 per year. It is a gold mine of detailed, up-to-the-minute travel information useful to all inveterate travelers, single or not.

For information: Travel Companion Exchange Inc., PO Box 833, Amityville, NY 11701; 800-392-1256 or 516-454-0880. Send $6 for a sample newsletter.

CONNECTING

A solo travel network, Connecting is a club based in Canada that sends its members a lengthy bimonthly newsletter, with a page devoted to mature travelers, that's full of advice on where to go, what to do, and how to enjoy your travels as a single. Special features include a free forum for travel companion ads to help members find others to wander with, reader recommendations, and a hospitality exchange. Members, who pay an annual fee of $30 (Canadian) or $25 (U.S.), also receive *The Single-Friendly Travel Directory*, a guide to travel companies with special accommodations or programs for solo travelers.

For information: Connecting, PO Box 29088, 1996 W. Broadway, Vancouver, BC V6J 5C2, Canada; 800-557-1757 or 604-737-7791.

PARTNERS FOR TRAVEL

Partners for Travel, with a few hundred members, provides a matchmaking service for independent single travelers, most of whom are in the Miami area. For a fee of $60 a year or $36 for six months, members receive an informative eight-page bimonthly newsletter and profiles of fellow members who are looking for travel mates. Contacts and travel arrangements are then up to you. The club also organizes and escorts tours, spa vacations, and cruises for single, divorced, or widowed men and women over 45. All singles, members or not, may participate in these events as well as an annual National Singlefest, a week of social networking.

For information: Partners for Travel, PO Box 560337, Miami, FL 33256; 305-279-8738.

TOURS FOR SOLO TRAVELERS

Most tour operators and agencies specializing in escorted trips for people in their prime will try to find you a room-mate (of the same sex) to share your room or cabin so you will not have to pay a single supplement. And, if they can't manage to find a suitable roommate, they will usually re-duce the supplement or even charge no single fee at all. Some run singles trips as well. In any case, keep in mind that you'll hardly have time or opportunity to be lonely on the typical escorted tour run by these agencies. If you are planning an extended stay in just one location, however, you may have more need for company.

For more about the tour operators listed below, see Chapter 5. Other companies may offer the same roommate-matching service, though they don't make a point of it, so always ask about it if you're interested.

BALLROOM DANCERS WITHOUT PARTNERS

This agency specializes in cruises for single men and women who like to travel and love to dance. There's no need to take a partner along because dance hosts see to it that you never lack for attention. If you want to share a cabin with another solo traveler and none are available, the cabin is yours alone at no additional cost. See Chapter 5.

For information: Ballroom Dancers Without Partners, 1449 NW 15th St., Miami, FL 33125; 800-778-7953 or 561-361-9384.

GOLDEN AGE TRAVELLERS

An over-50 club, Golden Age Travellers will enroll you in its "Roommates Wanted" list if you want help in finding a companion with whom to share the costs and the fun. See Chapter 5 for more information.

For information: Golden Age Travellers, Pier 27, The Embarcadero, San Francisco, CA 94111; 800-258-8880.

GRAND CIRCLE TRAVEL

Grand Circle, which concentrates on over-50 travel packages, tries to match singles with appropriate roommates if they request them. If there are none at hand, you will be charged only half the single supplement for your own room on most trips. And on several of its Live Abroad Vacations departure dates, you will not pay the single supplement at all. See Chapter 5 for more about Grand Circle.

For information: Grand Circle Travel, 347 Congress St., Boston, MA 02210; 800-248-3737 or 617-350-7500.

MATURE TOURS

Mature Tours specializes in travel for "youthful spirits" over the age of 50 who wish to roam the world with other mature travelers. A division of Solo Flights, which has a long history of catering to the single voyager, it welcomes both solo seniors and couples on its trips. Regular destinations include Costa Rica, Spain, and New York City. Also frequently on its schedule: steamboat cruises on the Mississippi River, some with add-on stays in New Orleans.

For information: Mature Tours, 10 Greenwood Lane, Westport, CT 06430; 800-266-1566 or 203-256-1235.

MAYFLOWER TOURS

Another travel operator with mature travelers as its focus, Mayflower will get you a roommate if you ask for one or, if that's not possible, absorb the cost of the single-room supplement. You'll then pay the regular twin rate.

For information: Mayflower Tours, 1225 Warren Ave., Downers Grove, IL 60515; 800-323-7604 or 708-960-3430.

MERRY WIDOWS DANCE TOURS

If you are a single woman over 50 who was born to dance, consider a trip with the Merry Widows. Known for its cruises, it also has land tours that transport you to exciting places on this continent and abroad, not only to dance but also to see the sights. If you're traveling alone, you'll be assigned a roommate if you want one. See Chapter 5 for more.

For information: Merry Widows Dance Tours, 1515 N. Westshore Blvd., Tampa, FL 33607; 800-374-2689.

PARTNERS FOR TRAVEL

A matchmaking agency for singles, Partners for Travel also organizes and escorts trips, tours, and cruises for solo travelers over 45 years old. More information earlier in this chapter.

For information: Partners for Travel, PO Box 560337, Miami, FL 33256; 800-866-5565 or 305-661-1878.

FOREVER YOUNG AT CLUB MED

The Forever Young program from **Club Med** gives travelers over 55 discounts at four of its villages all year except during major holidays. The locations were chosen because they have intensive sports programs, a nearby golf course, good shopping, and comfortable accommodations with few stairs or hills. Sign on for Caravelle in Guadeloupe, Columbus Isle or Paradise Island in the Bahamas, or Bora Bora in French Polynesia, and you'll get a reduction on your bill of $140 per person per week or $20 a day. The same applies to cruises aboard *Club Med 2*, a sailing ship that plies the Caribbean in the winter and the Mediterranean in the summer.

For information: Club Med, 800-CLUB MED (800-258-2633).

SAGA HOLIDAYS

Saga, well known for its holidays exclusively for travelers over the age of 50, schedules singles-only departures with no single supplements on many of its itineraries. That means lone participants pay no more per person than couples do. Not only that, but there is no extra charge or only a modest one for solo participants on many of its other tours all over the world.

Saga Holidays also tries to match travelers with roommates, if requested—another way to eliminate additional charges and also to provide companionship. It guarantees a roommate for land vacations or no extra charge if one is not available.

For information: Saga Holidays, 222 Berkeley St., Boston MA 02116; 800 343 0273.

SOLO FLIGHTS

This agency makes it its business to know about the best tours, cruises, packages, groups, and rates for single people of all ages, and will suggest where to go on short holidays or lengthy vacations here or abroad. It represents major tour operators and cruise lines and also offers its own package trips, some marketed by its affiliate, Mature Tours, exclusively for older travelers. One call or letter and you can find out what's out there that might possibly interest you. In return for the consultation, the agency hopes to do your booking.

For information: Solo Flights, 10 Greenwood Lane, Westport, CT 06880; 800-266-1566 or 203-256-1235.

HOOK-UPS FOR SOLO RVers

RVers who travel alone in their motor homes or vans can hook up with others in the same circumstances when they join one of the groups mentioned below. All of the clubs provide opportunities to travel together or to meet at campgrounds on the road, making friends with fellow travelers and having a fine time.

LONERS OF AMERICA

LOA is a club for single campers who want to travel together. Established in 1987, it currently has 29 chapters throughout the country and well over 800 active members from their 40s to their 90s, almost all retired and widowed, divorced, or otherwise single. Many of them live year-round in their motor homes or vans, and others hit the road only occasionally. They camp together, rally together, caravan together, often meeting at special campgrounds that cater to solo campers.

A not-for-profit member-operated organization, the club publishes a biannual membership directory and a lively monthly newsletter that keeps members in touch and informs them about campouts and rallies all over the country. The chapters organize their own events as well. Currently, dues are $30 a year plus a $5 registration fee for new members.

For information: Loners of America, PO Box 3314, Napa, CA 94558; 888-805-4562.

LONERS ON WHEELS

A camping and travel club for mature single campers, Loners on Wheels is not a lonely hearts club or a matchmaking service, but simply an association of friends and extended family. With about 65 chapters located throughout the United States and Canada, LOW now has a membership of about 2,800 unpartnered travelers. The club schedules hundreds of camping events during the year, at sites that are usually remote and/or primitive and cost little. A monthly newsletter and an annual directory keep everyone up to date and in touch. Annual dues at this writing are $36 U.S. and $45 Canada, plus a one-time enrollment fee of $5.

For information: Loners on Wheels, PO Box 1355, Poplar Bluff, MO 63902. Ask for a free sample newsletter.

FRIENDLY ROAMERS

Founded by former members of Loners on Wheels, Friendly Roamers is open to everyone, couples as well as singles, so friendships and RV activities can be continued despite a change of marital status or travel arrangements. Membership gets you admission to all club events, such as rallies and campouts, a newsletter, and a membership directory. Annual dues are $10 (plus a one-time registration fee of $5 for new members). Local chapters hold their own events and join the others as well.

For information: Friendly Roamers, PO Box 2010, Sparks, NV 89432.

S*M*A*R*T

An RV club for former members of the armed services, Special Military Active Retired Travel Club (S*M*A*R*T) sponsors caravans and musters for its 3,500 members in 42 chapters around the country and helps military bases improve their family campgrounds. Caravans have recently traveled to a variety of destinations, including the West, Arkansas, the Northwest, and Tennessee. To join, you must pay an initiation fee of $10, and then $25 a year per family.

For information: S*M*A*R*T Inc., 600 University Office Blvd., Pensacola, FL 32504; 800-354-7681.

RVing WOMEN

Women travelers who take to the highways in recreational vehicles can get advice and support from RVing Women, a club with over 4,000 female members. The group sponsors rallies, caravans, and other events across the U.S., Canada, and Mexico, plus weekend RV maintenance and RV driving classes in many locations around the country. Members pay an annual membership fee of $42 and receive a bimonthly magazine that covers topics such as safety,

scams on the road, vehicle maintenance, and announce-
ments of upcoming events and includes an annual directory of members.

For information: RVing Women, PO Box 1940, Apache
Junction, AZ 85217; 888-55-RVING (888-557-8464) or
602-983-4678.

7

Airfares: Improving with Age

ne thing that improves with age—yours—is air-fare. Almost every airline now offers senior coupon books, one of the best airfare deals today. The basic idea is simple: If you are 62 or over, you may buy the coupons, each good for a one-way trip within the lower 48 states and sometimes beyond. On long flights, they can save you a good deal of money.

As an alternative, almost every airline—both domestic and foreign—also gives senior travelers and a traveling companion of any age a flat 10 percent discount on most individual tickets, not much of a deal perhaps but better than nothing when you can't find a better fare. And one airline issues passes that allow seniors with wanderlust virtually unlimited travel at a fixed rate from a home city for a choice of four months or a year.

You get these nice offers because you, the mature population, have proved to be the hottest travel market around, a vast and growing group of careful consumers with money in your pockets and time on your hands midweek and in off-peak travel periods, just when the airlines are eager to fill up seats.

But, first, keep in mind:

■ Find a good travel agent and ask for the *lowest possible fare* to your destination at the time you want to fly. Mention the fact that you qualify for a senior discount, but be prepared to jump ship if you can get a better deal with a short-term sale rate or a supersaver fare—although sometimes your discount can cut these low fares even lower. Most airlines now offer promotional fares during off-peak seasons, sometimes specifically for seniors. Watch for these sales because they are usually the cheapest way to go, although in most cases you can't deduct the regular senior discount from them.

■ Keep in mind that the restrictions you must fly by may not be worth the savings. Always examine the fees and conditions and decide whether you can live with them. There may be blackout periods around major holidays when you can't use your privileges, departures only on certain days or hours, restrictions on the season of the year, or stiff penalties for flight changes. In some plans, you must travel the entire distance on one airline even if connections are poor. It's not always easy to sort out the offers.

■ Before you decide to buy Continental's four-month or yearly passport that lets you travel up to once a week, figure out how many trips you're likely to make during the next year. Unless you see clear savings, you are better off with individual tickets or coupon books. However, if you travel frequently, or would do so once you had the pass, then it could prove to be an excellent buy if you can live with the restrictions.

■ A 10 percent senior discount is obviously better than nothing, but on high-mileage trips you'll probably do much better with a coupon book if you fly often enough to use them up.

■ Try to couple your 10 percent senior discount with ultimate supersaver fares, which require 30-day advance purchase and include other restrictions.

■ Be prepared to present valid proof of age at the check-in counter. It's possible that your discount will not be honored if you don't have that proof with you, and you will have to pay the difference.

■ Virtually all airlines allow younger travel mates to fly with the same senior discount when you fly together for the entire trip.

■ Be flexible. To get the best fares when you use your senior discount, plan to fly at off-peak times, when the rest of the population isn't rushing off to faraway places. For example, noontime or late-night flights can be much cheaper than early-morning or dinnertime flights. Consider leaving on a different day—fares are often lower midweek or on Saturday. And obviously, flying off-season, when children aren't on vacation and there are no major holidays, may pay off with better prices.

■ Senior airline coupon books are one of the outstanding buys today, although their prices have been steadily rising. With coupons, a 62-plus traveler can go anywhere within the lower 48 states and sometimes beyond for much less than the regular coach fares for long trips, and sometimes less than promotional sale fares. There are no senior coupons for travel to Europe, Asia, or other overseas destinations. Each coupon is good for a one-way trip, including connecting flights as long as you don't stop over at a connection point. Two coupons are generally required each way for Alaska and Hawaii.

■ The coupons have many additional advantages. For example, unlike other low-fare tickets that require round-trip reservations, those you get with your coupons allow you to fly one way and decide later when you will return, so there's no minimum-stay requirement. You don't have to stay over a Saturday night and, in most cases, you must make your reservations only 14 days before departure. You may use them, too, with one exception, for instant travel on a standby basis, infinitely cheaper than the usual last-minute fares. With some exceptions, coupons for younger companions are not available, but you will get frequent-flyer mileage for the miles you fly. Each traveler requires a separate coupon book, which can't be shared with a spouse or anyone else, except on US Airways, where seniors may use their coupons for children under 12 who accompany them.

■ Eight-coupon books, now issued by only a couple of airlines, cost less per flight than four-coupon books. After you've used the first coupon in your book, the remaining vouchers become nonrefundable, so don't buy the books unless you are sure you will use them all. Once issued, the coupons must be redeemed for tickets and reservations made within a year, but in most cases you have another year to travel because you can book flights 12 months ahead. You may buy the booklets from your travel agent or the airline.

■ Remember that it costs the same for a few hundred miles as for several thousand, so don't waste your coupons on short trips. In other words, the longer the distance, the greater the savings. For shorter trips, you are probably better off with the 10 percent senior discount.

■ Book your flights as early as possible for the best fares and the most available seats. Seats for travel on senior coupons or senior discounts are limited and may not be issued at all on some flights.

■ If you want to join a private airline VIP club so you can spend waiting time at airports in peace and comfort, complete with snacks and free drinks, copy machines, private telephones, luggage storage areas, and sometimes even showers, remember that you can buy a lifetime membership at age 62 for about half the regular fee from many major airlines.

Now for some of the good deals awaiting you. Be advised that airfares and airline policies can change overnight—and often do—so always call the airline that interests you for an update.

U.S. AIRLINES
ALASKA AIRLINES
Fly on Alaska Airlines at 62-plus and you'll get 10 percent off almost all fares along with frequent-flyer credits. So will a traveling companion of any age.

For information: Call your travel agent or 800-426-0333.

AMERICA WEST AIRLINES

America West's Senior Saver Pack, for travelers 62 and over, is a booklet of four coupons, each to be traded for a one-way ticket within a year. Priced below those of most other airlines, the coupons allow you to fly wherever the airline and its commuter airline, America West Express, go within the U.S., Canada, and Mexico. However, travel days are limited. You may fly on coupon tickets only from Monday noon through Thursday noon and all day Saturday. And there are many blackout dates when you cannot use them. Flights to Anchorage require two coupons each way. Reservations must be made at least 14 days in advance, although standby is permitted.

America West also gives you and a younger companion a discount of 10 percent on the regular coach fares. But be sure to ask about the special senior fares offered on some flights—they may prove to be an even better buy.

For information: Call your travel agent or 800-235-9292.

AMERICAN AIRLINES

American Airlines has two good offers for passengers over 62. One is a 10 percent discount on any regular fare, even the lowest, for you and a traveling companion.

The other is its Senior TrAAveler Coupon Books, which give you four coupons per book. Traded in for a ticket, each coupon is good for travel one way in the continental U.S. as well as Puerto Rico and the U.S. Virgin Islands. Flights to Hawaii require two coupons each way.

You may travel any day of the week, but you must buy your tickets at least 14 days in advance of your flight or fly standby. There is no refund on the coupons and no change of itinerary on one-way tickets, although if you don't take your reserved flight, you may use the ticket for a standby seat. On round-trips, you may change your outbound flight at least 14 days before the flight for a $50 service charge. You may change your return anytime for a $50 service charge. Seats are limited, but you will be entitled to frequent-flyer credits for all the miles you fly. The same privileges apply to flights on American Eagle, AA's commuter airline affiliate.

Two other programs for travelers over 62 are no longer open for enrollment, although if you are already a member you will continue to receive their benefits. Lifetime members of the Senior SAAvers Club will continue to get its newsletter and a 10 percent discount on fares. Members of the AActive American Travel Club, for which enrollment has now closed, may also continue to take advantage of its offers, which include bargain airfares to both domestic and international destinations. They must, of course, continue to pay the annual fee of $40 a year for an individual or $60 for an individual plus a companion. This program may open its enrollment some time in the future.

For information: Call your travel agent or 800-433-7300 for reservations. For the Senior TrAAveler Coupon Books or the AActive American Travel Club, call 800-237-7981.

AMERICAN TRANS AIR (ATA)

A low-fare airline based in the Midwest, ATA flies primarily to vacation destinations—Florida, Las Vegas, Los Angeles, Phoenix, San Francisco, and the Caribbean. It offers a 10 percent discount to passengers over the age of 62.

For information: Call your travel agent or 800-435-9282.

ASPEN MOUNTAIN AIR/LONE STAR AIRLINES

This regional carrier flies out of Dallas/Fort Worth to many small Midwest cities. If you are over 62, it will give you special senior rates on most routes, so ask about them. But first find out if there's a current promotional fare that is even better.

For information: Call your travel agent or 800-877-3932.

CONTINENTAL AIRLINES

Continental Airlines offers some excellent deals for senior travelers and now gives you a choice of three options. First, there's the 10 percent discount on all fares, even the lowest, for you and a younger companion if you are at least 62. Simply ask for it and be ready to prove your age. You'll get mileage points.

The next choice is Freedom Trips, booklets of four or eight coupons, each to be traded for a one-way ticket on flights in the continental U.S., Canada, Mexico, the Caribbean, the Bahamas, Puerto Rico, and Bermuda. Two coupons are required for flights to Hawaii and Alaska. You must make reservations or changes at least 14 days in advance or travel standby. You may fly any day except during blackouts around major holidays—or fly standby—and you are entitled to frequent flyer points for the miles you fly. You must redeem your coupons within a year after purchase, but you have another year to complete your travel.

Continental is the only U.S. airline that offers a senior pass, the third choice for people over 62. This is the Freedom Passport, a great bargain if you like to be always on the move. For a flat fee, it allows you a single one-way flight once a week. The Domestic Freedom Passport, available for either four months or one year, permits travel one way once a week within mainland U.S. and Puerto Rico. Add-ons at a surcharge are yours for trips to Alaska, Hawaii, Canada, and foreign destinations. The Global Passport, more expensive, good for a year, covers travel in all 50 states plus Mexico, the Caribbean, Central America, and Europe.

A companion of any age may buy the same Passport you purchase at the same price. Travel is permitted between noon on Monday through noon on Thursday and all day Saturday and you must stay over a Sunday night. There are holiday blackouts and only a limited number of seats on each flight are made available for Passport holders. You are allowed a single one-way trip per week but will not earn mileage credits. You may travel to the same destination from your home city a maximum of three times.

Bonus: A lifetime membership in Continental's President Club will cost you, if you are at least 62, only half what it costs those who are younger.

For information: Call your travel agent or 800-523-FARE (800-523-3273) for reservations. For Freedom Passports or Freedom Trips, call 800-441-1135.

DELTA AIRLINES

At age 62, you have some good options from Delta. The first is a 10 percent discount on virtually all published fares, even including most sale fares, for you and a travel partner for flights within the continental U.S. and to Alaska, Hawaii, Puerto Rico, Canada, and the U.S. Virgin Islands. Seats are limited, so book early. Of course you'll be entitled to mileage points when you use the discount.

Your second choice is the Young at Heart Coupon program, which lets you purchase booklets of four coupons for a flat fee. The coupons must be traded within a year for tickets to any Delta city in the continental United States, Puerto Rico, the U.S. Virgin Islands, or Canada, with two coupons required for flights to Alaska or Hawaii. You may fly any day of the week and you'll get frequent flyer credits for your miles. Reservations and/or changes must be made at least 14 days before departure. Remember that only a limited number of seats are available for passengers using senior coupons, so plan ahead. Without reservations, you may travel standby any time.

Probably the best deal of all is Delta's Seniors Select Savings Plus program, a club with limited enrollment that features significant discounts on coach and first-class fares to any of 240 destinations served by Delta and Delta Connection in the continental U.S., Hawaii, and Alaska. Unfortunately, at this writing, enrollment in the club has closed. But you may have your name added to the waiting list for new members by calling the number below. No Saturday-night or minimum stay is required, nor are round-trip reservations, but tickets must be purchased at least 14 days in advance. Benefits also include savings on rental cars, vacation packages, cruises, and seasonal specials on flights to Europe and Canada. To become a member, you must be at least 62, pay an annual membership fee of $40, and belong to Delta SkyMiles, the airline's frequent-flyer plan. You may also enroll up to three companion members (adults over 62 or grandchildren aged 2 through 12) for an additional fee.

For information: Call your travel agent or 800-221-1212. For Seniors Select Savings Plus, call 800-325-3760.

DELTA SHUTTLE

On shuttle flights between New York and Washington, D.C., or Boston, you get the Senior Fare, currently half of the fare for other adults—that is, if you are 62 and can provide evidence of that fact a half hour before flight time. And you are eligible for frequent-flyer credits for your miles. With this fare, you must fly between 10:30 A.M. and 2:30 P.M. or 7:30 P.M. and 9:30 P.M. Monday through Friday or all day Saturday or Sunday. No reservations are required. Just show up at the gate.

A second option is the Senior Flightpack, four one-way tickets that must be used within a year on flights that leave in off-peak hours: 10:30 A.M. to 2:30 P.M. or 7:30 to 9:30 P.M. Monday through Friday and all day Saturday or Sunday. To be eligible for this good deal, you must be at least 62. Frequent-flyer credits apply. The Flightpack may be purchased only in a shuttle city—although you may buy a voucher through your travel agent and trade it for the booklet when you arrive at the airport.

For information: Call your travel agent or 800-221-1212.

HAWAIIAN AIRLINES

At age 60, you and a traveling companion are entitled to a 10 percent discount on some first-class and high-end coach fares on flights between the mainland and Honolulu. Ask about promotional fares before using the senior discount.

For information: Call your travel agent or 800-367-5320.

KIWI INTERNATIONAL AIR LINES

Serving the East Coast as well as Las Vegas and San Juan, Kiwi takes 10 percent off your fare, except on special promotions, for you at age 62 and a travelmate. It also sells a

Senior Discount Pack of six coupons good for one-way flights wherever the airline goes. Kiwi is the only airline that allows you and a companion traveling with you to use your coupons, which you will trade in for tickets. You must reserve within seven days of departure or fly standby any time. There are no fees for changing or cancelling your flights, and no need to stay over Saturday night or to be concerned about blackouts when coupons can't be used. *For information:* 800-JET-KIWI (800-538-5494).

MIDWAY AIRLINES

You and a travelmate of any age may take advantage of Midway's 10 percent senior discount if you are over 62. Or, at only 60, you may purchase the Senior Travel Coupon Booklet, a packet of four senior coupons redeemable for one-way travel to almost anywhere Midway or Midway Connection flies up and down the East Coast. For travel to Cancun, two coupons are required each way. To take along a travel companion of any age, you can purchase a Companion Coupon Booklet for only a few dollars more than yours. *For information:* Call your travel agent or 800-44-MIDWAY (800-446-4392).

MIDWEST EXPRESS

Ten percent is the discount on published fares for people over the age of 62 on Midwest Express, an airline that flies out of Milwaukee to many cities in the U.S. *For information:* Call your travel agent or 800-452-2022.

NORTHWEST AIRLINES

You and a companion of any age get a senior discount of 10 percent, complete with frequent-flyer credits, on most of Northwest's published fares when you've attained the age of 62. Going to Hawaii? As a senior, you may travel from island to island for $55 on Northwest's partner airline.

At the same age, you're also eligible to purchase NorthBest Senior Coupons, a booklet of four coupons, each good for a one-way flight within the lower 48 states and Canada and to Puerto Rico. Two coupons are required each way to Hawaii and Alaska. For stopovers, an additional coupon is required. Reservations must be made 14 days in advance, but you may fly any time, any day, and collect mileage credits. Or you may fly standby any time. Coupons must be traded for tickets within a year.

Bonus: a lifetime membership in Northwest Airlines World Club will cost you only about a third of what it costs those who are younger.

For information: Call your travel agent or 800-225-2525.

PAN AM AIRWAYS

This low-fare airline out of Florida gives passengers over 62 and a travelmate a discount of 10 percent off virtually all fares every day of the year.

It also offers over-60s its Senior Sampler Pack, four one-way flight coupons for travel between Florida and the Northeast. The coupon books are sold for a flat fee, guaranteeing the fare even during the high season. There are no minimum or maximum stays, penalties for changes, Saturday-night stays, or advance bookings required. The coupons must be traded within a year but they may also be used to travel standby if you want to take your chances on getting a seat at the last minute. Seats, of course, are limited and there are several blackout periods around major holidays throughout the year. Once ticketed, it will cost you $50 to change your

reservation. You may collect mileage points for your flights when you use either the coupons or the senior discount.
For information: Call your travel agent or 800-824-7386.

RENO AIR

A low-cost carrier, Reno Air serves over a dozen cities in the western U.S. and Canada, plus Chicago and Detroit, and gives passengers over 62 a discount of 10 percent off all posted fares, with deeper discounts on some routes. No advance purchase is necessary.
For information: Call your travel agent or 800-RENO AIR (800-736-6247).

SOUTHWEST AIRLINES

This airline that now flies throughout the United States offers travelers over 65 special senior fares that vary from city to city and change frequently on every flight every day. Reservations are required but advance purchase is not necessary. Tickets are fully refundable. However, seats per flight are limited, so you can't always get them when you want them. Besides, the senior fares may not always be the best buy. Ask for the best available fare.
For information: Call your travel agent or 800-I FLY SWA (800-435-9792).

TWA (TRANS WORLD AIRLINES)

TWA reduces the fare by 10 percent for travelers 62 and over and companions of any age on almost all flights in the U.S. and Puerto Rico and some to Europe and the Middle East as well. Ask for the discount when you make reservations. You are entitled to frequent-flyer mileage.

The Senior Travel Pak is another alternative for travelers 62 or older. This gives you four or eight one-way domestic coupons at bargain prices (if you use them for long trips). Each coupon may be exchanged for a one-way ticket on flights in the mainland United States and Canada, plus Puerto Rico and Mexico. Two coupons are required each way for trips to Hawaii. TWA's packets include discount certificates for a 20 percent reduction on a ticket to Europe, a $50 discount on a TWA Getaway Vacation package, and two upgrades on rental cars. You may travel any day of the week except around Thanksgiving and Christmas. Seats are limited so book yours early. Reservations must be made 14 days in advance, but you may travel standby anytime before your scheduled flight after you have traded your coupon for a ticket. You're entitled to mileage points.

TWA also issues companion four- or eight-coupon books, at a $100 surcharge, to be used when you and a younger travelmate fly together. All of the coupons must be used by the same person. The discount certificate for travel to Europe is included.

One more benefit of age: a lifetime membership in TWA's Ambassador Club costs you at 62 less than half what it costs those who are younger.

For information: Call your travel agent or 800-221-2000.

UNITED AIRLINES

United has three programs that benefit mature travelers. The first is a 10 percent discount at age 62 on excursion fares for you and any traveling companion. The discount also applies to United Express, selected fares from regional carriers, and all fares on the Shuttle by United.

The next good deal is the Silver TravelPac program for passengers over 62, which offers packets of four coupons at a flat fee, each coupon good for a one-way ticket within mainland United States, and to San Juan or Canada. Two coupons are required each way to Hawaii or Alaska (except from Seattle). They may be used for flights any day of the week, although there are blackouts during holiday seasons, and you must trade them for tickets within a year of the purchase date. Reservations must be made at least 14 days in advance, but you may use the coupons to fly standby. You'll get mileage credits for the miles you fly. Remember, seats at discounted fares are always limited, so plan ahead.

The third offer for mature travelers from UAL is United Silver Wings Plus, a travel club for seniors. You may join at age 55 and become eligible for many benefits, such as certificates from hotel, car, and cruise partners of over $2,500 in value. A lifetime membership costs $225, but your welcome gifts include three $50 certificates to use against future travel and one $100 certificate for travel to Europe, plus bonus miles. Sign up for two years at $75 and you will receive three $25 travel certificates to help pay for future trips and other credits. Members earn mileage credits and upgrades and receive a newsletter. They may also get certificates that allow them to buy round-trip upgrades.

At age 62, you and a companion get the 10 percent senior discount on all published fares, even discount fares, on United Airlines, United Express, and the Shuttle by United; on selected routes with international partners; and on some fares from regional carriers such as Air Canada and Mount Cook Airlines of New Zealand.

For information: Call your travel agent or 800-241-6522. For United Silver Wings Plus: 214-760-0022. For the Silver TravelPac: 800-633-6563.

SHUTTLE BY UNITED

Connecting 12 West Coast cities, the Shuttle by United gives passengers over 62 a discount of 10 percent on all flights. Reservations are required.
For information: Call your travel agent or 800-SHUTTLE (800-748-8853).

US AIRWAYS

You at age 62 and a travel companion at any age can count on a 10 percent discount on all US Airways fares, except special promotions.

This airline also offers passengers over 62 its Golden Opportunities Coupons. You may buy, at a flat fee, a book of four one-way coupons, each to be traded within a year for a ticket to any destination within the continental United States, Canada, Mexico, the U.S. Virgin Islands, and Puerto Rico, including flights on its commuter lines. Reservations must be made at least 14 days in advance, or you may travel standby anytime once a ticket has been issued. You may fly any day of the week and get mileage credits for your flights.

US Airways gives you two bonuses. The first is that as many as two of your grandchildren, ages 2 through 11, may fly on your coupons if they travel with you. The other is that a lifetime membership in the US Airways Club will cost you, at over 62, about a third less than what it costs those who are younger.

For information: Call your travel agent or 800-428-4322.

US AIRWAYS SHUTTLE

You may fly at approximately half fare on this airline's hourly shuttle flights between New York and Boston or Washington, D.C., if you are 62 and are willing to travel at off-peak hours. You may fly Monday through Friday at the senior rate from 10:00 A.M. to 2:00 P.M., after 7:00 P.M., or any time Saturday or Sunday. No reservations are required.
For information: Call your travel agent or 800-428-4322.

VIRGIN ATLANTIC AIRWAYS

As soon as you turn 60, whoever you are, Virgin Atlantic gives you and a younger companion a 10 percent discount on all regular fares on all flights between the U.S. and London.

But if you are a member of AARP, you—and your spouse or a companion—can now save anywhere from 12 to 25 percent on all advance purchase (apex) and higher economy fares to London, although not in addition to other promotional offers or discounts. When making a reservation, be sure you or your travel agent mentions the AARP offer. Be ready to present your membership card when you check in for your flight. The discounts are not applicable for a few weeks around Easter and Christmas/New Year's holidays. As a member, you can also save $50 on the airline's vacation packages, except on promotional sales, to Great Britain and beyond.
For information: Call your travel agent or 800-862-8621

for reservations. Call 888-YES-VIRGIN (888-937-8474) for vacation packages.

GOOD DEALS ON CANADIAN AIRLINES

AIR CANADA

If you are over 60, you and any traveling companion are eligible for a 10 percent reduction on fares in both economy and business class, even including some special promotional sales, for flights in Canada and the U.S., including Florida. And on trips between Canada and the U.K. and the Caribbean. You'll get mileage credits as well.

In addition, at age 62 you and a companion can get the same discount on joint Air Canada flights with Continental and United Airlines.

For information: Call your travel agent or 800-776-3000 in the U.S.

CANADIAN AIRLINES INTERNATIONAL

The Canadian Golden Discount for passengers 60 or over gives you and a traveling companion of any age a 10 percent reduction on all round-trip fares on Canadian Airlines and all of its partners to destinations in Canada and the continental U.S., Mexico and the U.K., and on certain fares to Hawaii. You get frequent-flyer credits for your mileage, and there are no special restrictions on time, day, or season.

For information: Call your travel agent or 800 426-7000 in the U.S.; 800-665-1177 in Canada.

GOOD DEALS ON FOREIGN AIRLINES

Again, always inquire about special senior discounts when you book a flight, even if you don't see them listed here. Airlines change their policies with very little notice. Your travel agent can provide current information. Remember, too, that seasonal promotional fares available to all travelers can often be much lower than the fare you can get with your senior discount, so do your homework before committing yourself.

AEROLINEAS ARGENTINAS

On this airline, passengers over the age of 60 are offered a 10 percent discount on posted fares for flights originating in the United States to any of its South American destinations.

For information: Call your travel agent or 800-333-0276.

AEROLITORAL

A commuter airline operated by Aeromexico that flies from several cities in the U.S. Southwest to Mexico, Aerolitoral offers a 10 percent discount on its regular economy fares to passengers over 62.

For information: Call your travel agent or 800-237-7113.

AEROMEXICO

It's 10 percent off the regular first-class or tourist fares every day on all Aeromexico routes, domestic and international, if you are over 62.

For information: Call your travel agent or 800-237-6639.

AIR FRANCE

A 10 percent discount is yours at age 62 on Air France flights between major U.S. gateway cities and France. The discount also applies to a traveling companion who may be younger, and it is deducted from almost every fare, including the Concorde, except for special promotional sales. *For information:* Call your travel agent or 800-237-2747.

AIR JAMAICA

Fly to Jamaica in the off-peak season, which usually means spring and fall, and you can take advantage of Air Jamaica's 20 percent discount offered to passengers over the age of 60 on flights between the U.S. and Jamaica. Fly in a peak period and you'll get a 10 percent discount. Either way, a younger traveling companion gets the same discount you do. You must travel first class or economy on Tuesdays, Wednesdays, or Thursdays, plus Saturdays on flights between Miami or Fort Lauderdale and Jamaica. If you cancel your trip after ticketing, you will be charged a $25 service fee. *For information:* Call your travel agent or 800-523-5585.

ALITALIA

When you fly on Alitalia to its European destinations or Egypt, you qualify for a 10 percent discount when you are 62, as does a younger traveling companion. When you travel on an advance-purchase fare via Alitalia from the U.S. to Israel, you will get a 15 percent discount if you are 60. So will your companion if he or she accompanies you and is at least 55.

On certain domestic flights within Italy, seniors over 65 are offered special discounted Terza Eta (Third Age) fares. Be sure to ask for them.

For information: Call your travel agent or 800-223-5730.

BRITISH AIRWAYS

The good deal from British Airways for travelers over 60 and a companion is a discount of 10 percent on all advance-purchase economy-class airfares on trips from all 21 gateway cities in the U.S. and the three gateways in Canada to the U.K. and Europe. Also there is no charge for cancelling or changing your flights if you make your changes before your initial departure. A tip: Ask about the All Seasons Apex Fare, for which tickets must be purchased 90 days or more in advance of departure. It may save you more money than your senior discount. Keep your eyes open, too, for the occasional World Offers, special sales that can be very good deals.

For information: Call your travel agent or 800-247-9297.

CAYMAN AIRWAYS

This small airline that flies from Miami, Tampa, or Houston to the Cayman Islands will take 10 percent off your fare, except for sale fares, if you are 62.

For information: Call your travel agent or 800-422-9626.

EL AL ISRAEL AIRLINES

Travelers over the age of 60 and their spouses over 55 are entitled to El Al's senior fare, which gives you a discount of about 15 percent off the regular Apex fare between the U.S. and Israel. You may stay for up to two months, a 14-

day advance purchase is required, and there is a $50 fee for changing your return flight.

But, before accepting this deal, check out the cheaper Superapex fare with its maximum stay of 45 days. It may work out better for you. And don't forget to look into El Al's economical Israel Milk and Honey Vacation packages, available only with a round-trip ticket from the U.S. to Tel Aviv.

Traveling with your grandchildren? If they are under 12, the first one flies at 25 percent off, the second at 50 percent off, and the third at 75 percent off.

For information: Call your travel agent or 800-223-6700.

FINNAIR

On flights between gateway cities in the U.S. and Canada and Helsinki, Finland, you will get a 10 percent reduction off the regular economy fares if you are 65 years old or more. Travel companions of any age get the same discount. You'll get an even better discount—a whopping 70 percent—on Finnair's domestic flights in Finland. You must be 65 and pay for your tickets within three days of booking.

For information: Call your travel agent or 800-950-5000.

IBERIA AIRLINES OF SPAIN

Iberia gives you 10 percent off regular published fares for transatlantic flights originating in North America, except on special sales. You must have reached 62 to get the privilege, but you may take a younger companion who pays the same fare.

For information: Call your travel agent or 800-772-4642.

KLM ROYAL DUTCH AIRLINES

KLM's discount for people over the age of 62 is 10 percent on all nonpromotional fares between the U.S. and its European destinations. Flying on KLM to Paris from the U.S., your discount is even better—30 percent. A companion of any age is entitled to the same reduction in fare if you travel together for the entire journey.

For information: Call your travel agent or 800-374-7747.

LACSA AIRLINES

Flying from the U.S. to many destinations in Central and South America, Costa Rica's Lacsa Airlines gives travelers over 55 departing from Miami or Orlando a special senior rate. From other gateway cities—New Orleans or San Francisco—the discount is 10 percent off the fares at 55. From New York or Los Angeles, you must be 62 to qualify for the same reduction.

For information: Call your travel agent or 800-225-2272.

LUFTHANSA

At age 60, you can get a 10 percent reduction on most fares, including first-class, business, and economy, for yourself and another adult (over 18) travelmate, on Lufthansa flights to and from the U.S. and Germany. Seats are limited and you must request the discount when you make your reservations.

For information: Call your travel agent or 800-645-3880.

MARTINAIR HOLLAND

Martinair Holland, "the other Dutch airline," flies from nine North American gateway cities to Amsterdam and other European destinations. To travelers over 60 (and younger companions) it offers a one-year stay on its lowest published fares, an open return that eliminates penalties for changes, and waived advance-purchase requirements.

For information: Call your travel agent or 800-MARTIN-AIR (800-627-8462).

MEXICANA AIRLINES

A senior discount of 10 percent applies to most Mexicana international flights between gateway cities in the U.S. or Canada and Mexico. You must be 62, but your traveling companion may be younger and get the same rate.

For information: Call your travel agent or 800-531-7921.

SABENA BELGIAN WORLD AIRLINES

At 62, you are entitled to a 10 percent discount on all fares except promotional packages from the United States to Belgium and via Brussels to other Sabena destinations in Europe. For an even better deal, look into Sabena's Eurostarters, low-cost packages. Available all year, their lowest fares are offered November through March. In addition, Sabena offers special senior fares to travelers over 60 and spouses over 55 on round-trip flights to Israel. You must stay a minimum of six days and a maximum of two months and book a week in advance. Bonus: one free stopover in the United States and another in Europe on your way to or from Tel Aviv.

For information: Call your travel agent or 800-955-2000.

SAS (SCANDINAVIAN AIRLINES SYSTEM)

Flying SAS across the Atlantic Ocean from U.S. gateway

cities to Scandinavia and European destinations, you will get a 10 percent reduction on most fares if you are 62 or older.

On all flights within Norway, SAS offers a 50 percent discount to passengers of all nationalities who are 65 and over. Tickets must be purchased in Norway. Within Denmark, you are entitled to a senior discount of 10 percent on certain fares depending on the routing, but for this you must wait until you are 65. And on domestic flights in Sweden, there are special senior citizen fares for passengers 65 and over.

For information: Call your travel agent or 800-221-2350.

SWISSAIR

Swissair offers two good options to travelers over the age of 62 (in Canada, that's 60) and their younger traveling companions. One is a 10 percent discount on almost all published fares on flights from its 10 U.S. and Canadian gateway cities to destinations in Europe. Yours for the asking, it is available on flights all year round and every day of the week.

The second deal from this airline is a 10 percent discount for you and a companion, up to $100 per person, when you book a Swissair land package.

For information: Call your travel agent or 800-221-4750. For the land program, call Swisspak, 800-688-7947.

TAP AIR PORTUGAL

Your discount from this airline if you are at least 62 is 10 percent off almost any fare on flights between the United

States and Portugal, Madeira, and the Azores. The discount applies to a younger flying partner as well. Watch for TAP's occasional special packages for seniors.

For information: Call your travel agent or 800-221-7370.

VARIG BRAZILIAN AIRLINES

On Varig's flights, there's a 10 percent discount for seniors only on full-fare tickets.

For information: Call your travel agent or 800-468-2744.

8

Beating the Costs of Car Rentals

Never rent a car without getting a discount or a special promotional rate. Almost all car-rental agencies in the United States and Canada give them to all manner of customers, including those who belong to over-50 organizations (see Chapter 19) or have reached a certain birthday. The discount that's coming to you as a senior member of society can save you some money, although short-term sales will almost always save you more. Refer to the membership material sent by the group to which you belong for information about your discount privileges.

But, first, keep in mind:
- Car-rental agents may not always volunteer information about senior discounts or special sales, so always ask for it when you reserve your car.
- Don't settle for a senior discount or senior rate too hastily without investigating the possibility of an even better

deal. Shop around yourself or ask your travel agent to find the *lowest available rate or package* at the time you are going to travel, and don't forget to ask about airport fees, taxes, and other extra charges. Senior discounts are usually given on the full published rental rate. So special promotional rates—in other words, sales—or even weekend rates are almost always better, sometimes much better. On the other hand, if you can get the senior discount *on top of the lowest posted rate*, regular or promotional, that's the deal you want. Thrifty, for example, guarantees a 10 percent discount off the lowest available rate.

■ When you reserve a car, always ask for a confirmation number. When you pick up your car, remember to verify the discount and ask if a better rate has become available since you booked.

■ When you call to ask about rates or reservations, always be armed with your organization's ID number and your own membership card for reference. Present them again at the rental counter when you pick up your car and remember to confirm your rate before signing the agreement.

■ Special savings may not be available at every location, so you need to remember to check them out every time you make a reservation.

■ Review your personal auto insurance coverage to determine if you require the optional loss/damage coverage offered by the rental companies.

■ If you want to rent a car in Europe, be sure to ask the rental agency if it imposes age restrictions on drivers. These vary by country and agency. One agency, for example, denies rentals to people over 65 in Greece and Northern Ireland, or over 75 in Ireland and Israel. In the

United Kingdom and Ireland, most agencies will not rent a car to a driver over 75. So make your age clear when you make your reservation. Shop around, and also consider leasing a car, in which case age may not be an issue.

ADVANTAGE RENT-A-CAR

Concentrated in the southwestern states, Advantage gives a 5 percent discount to members of AARP.
For information: Call your travel agent or 800-777-5500.

ALAMO RENT A CAR

The Senior Citizen Discount for anyone over the age of 50 takes 10 percent off the lowest available retail rate for weekly rentals and 3 percent off daily rentals of compact cars and up. A 24-hour advance reservation is required and so is a request for the senior discount.
For information: Call your travel agent or 800-GO-ALAMO (800-462-5266).

AVIS RENT-A-CAR

If you are a member of AARP, CARP, or Mature Outlook, you'll get a discount of 5 to 20 percent, sometimes more, on Avis rentals. The amount of the discount depends on factors such as destination, time of year, and length of your rental.
For information: Call your travel agent or 800-331-1800.

BUDGET RENT-A-CAR

If you are 50 years old and a member of a senior organization, you'll get 10 percent off Budget's standard rental rates in the U.S. and Canada.
For information: Call your travel agent or 800-527-0700.

DOLLAR RENT A CAR

The Silver Dollar Club gives anybody over the age of 50 a small discount that varies by location.

For information: Call your travel agent or 800-800-4000.

ENTERPRISE RENT-A-CAR

AARP and CARP members are entitled to 10 percent off the regular rental rates for all cars at Enterprise.

For information: Call your travel agent or 800-RENT-A-CAR (800-736-8222).

HERTZ CAR RENTAL

If you are a member of AARP, Mature Outlook, Y.E.S., or the National Association of Retired Federal Employees, you are entitled to savings, usually from 5 to 15 percent, on Hertz rental cars.

For information: Call your travel agent or 800-654-3131.

KEMWEL HOLIDAY AUTOS

A major tour operator in Europe, KHA also has arrangements with car-rental suppliers in many cities in the U.S.—mainly in California, Florida, and Texas—as well as some in Canada and the Caribbean. To be eligible for a 5 percent discount on the regular rates, you must have reached the age of 50 on this side of the Atlantic Ocean or 65 in Europe.

For information: Call your travel agent or 800-678-0678.

NATIONAL CAR RENTAL

With this rent-a-car agency, you'll get discounts—from 10 to 30 percent—that vary by destination, car class, and time of year on all rentals if you are a member of AARP, CARP, or Mature Outlook.

For information: Call your travel agent or 800-227-7368.

PAYLESS CAR RENTAL

Mature travelers—50 and over—get a straightforward 5 percent discount off the lowest applicable rate when they've signed up for the Nifty 50 program. It's free. Join at any location or by calling the number below.

For information: Call your travel agent or 800-PAYLESS (800-729-5377).

THRIFTY CAR RENTAL

Now here's a really good deal: if you are 55 or more, Thrifty guarantees you a 10 percent discount off its lowest available rates, *including* promotional sale rates, at all of its locations in the U.S. and Canada. So shop for the best price, then add your senior discount before you make your reservation.

For information: Call your travel agent or 800-367-2277.

9

Saving a Bundle on Trains, Buses, and Boats in North America

Getting around town, especially in a city where driving is not a practical option, probably means depending on public transportation to get you from hither to yon. Remember that, once you reach a particular birthday—in most cases, your 60th or 65th—you can take advantage of some good senior markdowns on trains, buses, subways and, in some places, even taxis. All you usually need is a Medicare card, a Senior ID card, or your driver's license to play this game, which usually reduces fares by half. Although you may find it uncomfortable at first to pull out that card and flash it at the bus driver or ticket agent, it soon becomes very easy. Do it and you'll realize some nice savings.

And don't fail to take advantage of the bargains available to seniors on long-distance rail, bus, and boat travel as well.

RIDING THE RAILS

Probably every commuter railroad in the United States and Canada gives older riders a break, although you may have to do your traveling during off-peak periods when the trains are not filled with go-getters rushing to and from their offices. Ask for your discount when you purchase your ticket.

As for serious long-distance travel, many mature travelers are addicted to the railroads, finding riding the rails a leisurely, relaxed, romantic, comfortable, economical, and satisfying way to make miles while enjoying the scenery.

So many passes and discounts on railroads are available to travelers heading for other parts of the country that sorting them out becomes confusing. But, once you do, they will help stretch your dollars while you cover a lot of ground.

See Chapter 4 for the best deals on transportation in foreign countries for travelers of a certain age.

AMTRAK

To accommodate senior travelers, Amtrak offers a 15 percent discount on the lowest available coach fares, including All Aboard America Passes, and on some Canadian routes, every day of the week to anyone over 62. The discount is also available on the Metroliner Service on Saturdays and Sundays but does not apply to the Auto Train or sleeping accommodations. Consider taking your grandchildren with you because, up to age 15, they ride at 50 percent of the regular adult fare.

The lowest coach fares often sell out quickly, so try to book early. Not all fares are available on every train and

some have restrictions that may not suit your plans, which means you should always ask questions before you buy.
For information: Call Amtrak at 800-USA-RAIL (800-872-7245).

ALASKA RAILROAD

Passengers over 65 are entitled to a 25 percent reduction in weekend fares during the winter months—late September through mid-May—between Anchorage and Fairbanks and anywhere in between. Remember to take food and drink with you. There's no food service on the train for this 12-hour journey.
For information: Call Alaska Railroad at 800-544-0552.

VIA RAIL CANADA

The government-owned Canadian passenger railroad offers you, at age 60, 10 percent off the regular coach fare every day of the year with no restrictions. Add this 10 percent to the 40 percent reduction on off-peak travel, available to all ages and applicable any day of the week except Friday and Sunday, and you end up with tickets that are half price. Tickets at the off-peak rate must be purchased at least five or seven days in advance. However, the number of seats sold at this rate is limited, so plan ahead and buy your tickets as early as possible.

When you reach the age of 60, you are also eligible to buy a Canrailpass at a 10 percent discount. The pass allows you to travel for any 12 days during a 30-day period anywhere on Via Rail's transcontinental system. You may board and deboard the train as many times as you wish, stopping wherever you like along the way.

For information: Via Rail Canada, PO Box 8116, Station A, Montreal, QE H3C 3N3. For reservations or a Canrailpass, call your travel agent.

GOING BY BUS

Never, never board a bus without asking the driver whether there's a senior discount, because even the smallest bus lines in the tiniest communities (and the largest—New York City, for example) in this country and abroad give seniors a break, usually half fare at age 60 or 65. In Europe, your senior rail pass is often valid on major motorcoach lines as well, so always be sure to ask.

GREYHOUND BUS LINES

When Greyhound does the driving, you are entitled to a 10 percent reduction on any last-minute "walk up" fares if you have passed your 55th birthday. Be prepared to show a photo ID with proof of age. It pays to plan ahead, however, because advance-purchase fares are usually a much better deal than what you'll get with your senior discount, and sometimes there are special sales that are even better than those. For example, the periodic Companion Travels Free promotion that lets you ride at half price if you travel with someone else. By the way, seniors over 55 also get a 10 percent discount on Greyhound's Ameripass, which gives you unlimited travel for 7, 15, or 30 days to any U.S. destinations.

For information: Call your local Greyhound reservation office or 800-231-2222.

GREYHOUND CANADA

Here you'll get 10 percent off all regular fares, any day of the week, all year around, if you are a traveler over 60 with a valid ID. What's more, if you're accompanied by a younger companion and buy your tickets seven days in advance, the companion travels for half the senior fare. The 10 percent discount also applies to the Canadapass, which is good for unlimited travel for specified numbers of days.
For information: Call Greyhound Canada, 800-661-8747 or 403-265-9111.

GRAY LINE TOURS

Gray Line is an association of many small independent motorcoach lines in the U.S., Canada, and other parts of the world, that offers sight-seeing and package tours. Most, but not all, of them give a 10 percent discount on half- or full-day sight-seeing tours to members of AARP at age 50 and sometimes other seniors as well.
For information: Call your travel agent or the Gray Line Tours office in your area.

ONTARIO NORTHLAND

This passenger railroad serving northeastern Ontario gives travelers over the age of 60 a 25 percent fare reduction any day of the year. The lower fare applies on both the Northlander train that runs between Toronto and Cochrane and the Polar Bear Express, a summer excursion line between Cochrane and Moosonee, close to the Arctic Circle.
For information: Ontario Northland, 65 Front St. West, Toronto, ON M5J 1E6; 800-268-9281 or 416-314-3750.

TRENTWAY WAGAR

This bus line, which serves southwest Ontario and the Niagara Peninsula and runs between Toronto and Montreal, offers discounts ranging from 10 to 25 percent to passengers over the age of 60. In cooperation with Greyhound (U.S.), it also offers through service to Boston, New York, Washington, and Chicago.

For information: Trentway Wagar, 791 Webber Ave., Peterborough ON K9J 7A5; 800-461-7661 or 705-748-6411.

VOYAGEUR COLONIAL LTD.

This Canadian motorcoach line's Club 60 offers you a discount of 25 percent on all regular one-way bus fares throughout the provinces of Quebec and Ontario, without prior reservations, seven days a week. Simply present proof of your age when you buy your tickets.

For information: Voyageur Colonial Ltd.; 514-842-2281 in Montreal; 613-238-5900 in Ottawa.

GOING BY BOAT

ALASKA MARINE HIGHWAY

Traveling on the Alaska Marine Highway off-season is a bargain for foot passengers 65 and older. Between October and April, you sail for half the regular adult fare within Alaskan waters. The discount does not apply to vehicle or cabin space. Sometimes in the summer, too, there are half fares for seniors on several of the smaller vessels. The message is: always ask if a senior rate is available.

For information: Call 800-642-0066.

TOURING BY BOAT, RAIL, BUS
THE ALASKAPASS

With an AlaskaPass, you may travel on many kinds of surface transportation in Alaska and the Yukon Territory for a specified number of days, using gateways in British Columbia and the state of Washington. One set discounted price allows unlimited travel on participating ferries, buses, and trains. These include the Alaska Marine Highway ferries, the Alaskan Express Motorcoaches, the Alaska Railroad, Alaska Direct Bus Line, B.C. Rail, Laidlaw Coach Lines, Gray Lines of Seattle, Greyhound Canada, and Norline Coaches (Yukon). You plan your own itinerary, make your own reservations, and pay for your transportation with the pass, using, if you like, suggested itineraries. If you are planning a trip, you may wish to send for the *AlaskaPass Handbook* ($5), which provides itineraries, lodging information, schedules, and general information for independent travelers.

The off-season—September 15 through May 15—is when all travelers, especially seniors, get a good deal on the cost of the pass. Then, if you are over 65, an AlaskaPass Travelpass costs you $100 less than the discounted off-peak adult fare.

For information: Call your travel agent or AlaskaPass at 800-248-7598. For the AlaskaPass Handbook, send $5 to AlaskaPass, PO Box 351, Vashon, WA 98070.

10

Hotels and Motels: Get Your Over-50 Markdowns

Now that you're past 50, you'll never have to pay full price for a hotel room again. Across the United States and Canada, and often in the rest of the world today, virtually all lodging chains and most individual establishments go out of their way to give you a break on room rates.

You don't even have to wait until you're eligible for Social Security to cash in on your maturity because most hotels, inns, and motels offer discounts to you at age 50, usually requiring only proof of age or membership in a senior organization. Often the best discounts, sometimes as high as 50 percent, however, are reserved at some hotel chains for members of their own senior travel clubs. Some cost little or nothing to join; others charge a yearly fee.

What all this means is that you should *never* make a lodging reservation without making sure you are getting a special rate—a senior discount of at least 10 percent or an even better deal, such as a promotional sale or weekend rate that is lower. Always ask for the senior discount, whether or not one is posted or mentioned in the hotel's literature, and then ask if a better rate is available.

But, first, keep in mind:

If you want to take advantage of the privileges coming to you because of your age, you must do some advance research and planning with your travel agent or on your own.

- In this rapidly changing world, rates and policies can be altered in a flash, so an update is always advisable.
- Information about discounts is seldom volunteered. In most cases, you must arrange for discounts when you make your reservations and confirm them again when you check in. Do not wait until you're settling your bill because then it may be too late. Some hotels and motels require that you make advance reservations to get their discounts. "Advance" may mean a considerable period of time such as three weeks, but it may also mean only a week, a day, or even a few hours. Check it out before making your plans.
- Although many senior discounts are available every day of the year, some are subject to "space availability." This means it may be pretty hard to get them when you want to travel because only a limited number of rooms may be reserved for special rates. If these are already booked (or are expected to be booked), you won't get your discount. And some hotels have "blackout" dates during special events or holiday periods when the discount is

not valid. So always book early, ask for your discount privileges, and try to be flexible on your dates in order to take advantage of them. Your best bets for space are usually weekends in large cities, weekdays at resorts, and non–holiday seasons.

■ It's quite possible that a special promotional rate, especially off-peak or on weekends, may save you more money than your senior discount. Many hotels, particularly in big cities and warm climates, cut their prices drastically in the summer, for example. Others that cater mostly to businesspeople during the week try to encourage weekend traffic by offering bargain rates if you stay over a Saturday night. Resorts are often eager to fill their rooms on weekdays. So always investigate all the possibilities before you get too enthusiastic about using your hard-earned senior discount, and remember to ask for the *lowest available rate*.

■ There are several chains of no-frills budget motels that may not offer discounts or too much in the way of amenities but do charge very low room rates and tend to be located along the most-traveled routes.

■ In some cases, not every hotel or inn in a chain will offer the discount. Those that do are called "participating" hotels/motels. Make sure the one you are planning to visit is participating in the senior plan.

■ In addition to the chains, many independent hotels and inns are eager for your business and offer special reduced rates. Always *ask* before making a reservation. Your travel agent should be able to help you with this.

■ Some hotel restaurants will give you a discount too, sometimes whether or not you are a registered guest.

■ By the way, your discount usually applies only to the regular rates and, in most cases, will not be given on top of other special discounts. One discount is all you get.

AMERIHOST INN

At these motels concentrated in the Midwest, there's a senior discount of 10 percent on the rates.
For information: Call 800-434-5800.

AMERISUITES

These all-suite accommodations designed for extended stays offer members of AARP a 10 percent discount off the regular rates.
For information: Call 800-982-6374.

ASTON HOTELS & RESORTS

Aston's Sun Club gives travelers 50 and older—and their roommates—up to 25 percent off room rates at its hotels and condominium resorts on Hawaii's four major islands, plus special rates on car rentals. Ask for them when you make your reservations and pick up a coupon book of discounts when you check in. Sun Club rooms are limited, so reserve early.
For information: Call 800-922-7866.

BEST INNS

At these inexpensive inns mainly in the Midwest and South, anyone over 50 gets $5 discounts weekdays, $10 Sunday nights.
For information: Call 800-237-8466.

BEST WESTERN INTERNATIONAL

Just show your AARP or CARP membership card or prove you're over 55, and you will get a 10 percent savings on the rates every day of the year at every Best Western in the world. You will also be entitled to at least two special amenities at each hotel. These may include a complimentary continental breakfast, free local phone calls, a free newspaper, a room upgrade, late checkout, or other local offerings that may change by the season.

For information: Call 800-528-1234.

BUDGET HOST INNS

A network of about 200 affiliated, mostly family-owned economy inns in 41 states and Canada, most Budget Host Inns offer senior discounts—usually 10 percent—that vary by location. They may be confirmed when you make your reservation or check in. When you call the toll-free reservation number, you will be transferred directly to the front desk of the inn in which you want to stay so you may ask as many questions as you like about such matters as the accommodations, facilities, rates, discounts, and directions to the property.

For information: Call 800-283-4678.

BUDGETEL INNS

At these inexpensive motels located mainly in the South and Midwest, you will get a 10 percent discount just for being over 55. You will get it at 50 if you are a member of AARP.

For information: Call 800-428-3438.

AMERICAN EXPRESS SENIOR CARD

A charge card especially for retirees, the Senior Member Card from American Express provides a program of benefits and services. It gives you the usual American Express charge privileges and customer services, plus a quarterly newsletter and savings on travel, shopping, and dining. The Senior Global Assist Hotline is available 24 hours a day. Through it, members can get medical or legal referrals, get rush replacements on prescriptions and eyeglasses, or send emergency messages to family or friends. The Pharmacist on Call Hotline, open from 8 A.M. until 1 A.M. seven days a week, puts you in touch with a pharmacist who answers questions about medications. If you are over 62, you pay a reduced annual membership fee of $35 for the standard Senior Member Card or $55 for a Gold Senior Member Card.

For information: Call 800-THE CARD (800-843-2273).

CAMBERLEY HOTELS

Most of these charming upscale hotels, some of them members of Historic Hotels of America, give AARP members 10 percent off the standard room rates.

For information: Call 800-555-8000.

CANADIAN PACIFIC HOTELS & RESORTS

These grand hotels and resorts throughout Canada give a 30 percent discount on regular room rates, subject to availability, to card-carrying members of AARP and CARP. And some hotels offer more—a 20 percent reduction—to guests over 65.

Also, be sure to check out the special off-peak packages designed for older travelers at many Canadian Pacific hotels. For example: the Seniors Spring Fling, the Seniors

Fall Getaway, the Sixty-Something room rate, and the Second Honeymoon.
For information: Call 800-441-1414.

CASTLE RESORTS & HOTELS
With a collection of 21 budget, moderate, and deluxe hotels and resort condominiums on all five Hawaiian islands, the Castle Group offers you and your party a really good deal if you are at least 50 years old. It is a discount of up to 25 percent on the regular room rates, plus an air-conditioned subcompact car with unlimited mileage for an extra $29 a day.
For information: Call 800-367-5004.

CHOICE HOTELS
Choice Hotels is an international group of more than 4,000 inns in 33 countries with brand names that include Clarion, Comfort, Quality, Sleep, Econo Lodge, MainStay Suites, and Rodeway. All of its properties in the U.S. and Canada take catering to older travelers very seriously and offer their Senior Saver Discounts to anyone over the age of 50. This means you will get 30 percent taken off the regular room rate when you make an advance reservation using the toll-free number. Because only a limited number of rooms is set aside for this program, it pays to plan ahead. Without a reservation, your discount is 10 percent any day of the year.
For information: Call your travel agent or 800-4 CHOICE (800-424-6423).

CLARION HOTELS & RESORTS
See Choice Hotels. Call 800-CLARION (800-252-7466).

CLUBHOUSE INNS

A small group of inns mainly in the Midwest, ClubHouse Inns gives a 10 percent discount on published room rates to guests over 62. A unique extra benefit: a free night (with at least one paid night) the day before or the day after major holidays. A full breakfast buffet and evening beverage receptions are included.

For information: Call 800-CLUB-INN (800-258-2466).

COLONY HOTELS & RESORTS

Virtually all of Colony's hotels and condominium hotels in the United States and its resorts in the Caribbean give a 25 percent discount every day of the year to AARP members. Nonmembers who are over 60 get a discount of 20 percent. Advance reservations are a must.

For information: Call 800-777-1700.

COMFORT INNS

See Choice Hotels. Call 800-228-5150.

CONRAD INTERNATIONAL HOTELS

A subsidiary of Hilton Hotels Worldwide, many Conrad Hotels in Europe, Australia, Mexico, Hong Kong, and the Caribbean participate in Hilton's Senior HHonors Worldwide program for over-60s. Members are entitled to up to 50 percent off room rates and 30 percent off the bill for dinner for two. For more information, see Hilton Hotels.

COUNTRY HEARTH INNS

These economy motels in the South take 10 percent off the room rates for visitors over 50.

For information: Call 800-848-5767.

COUNTRY INNS & SUITES

These upper-economy inns all over the world give you a minimum of 10 percent off the regular rates if you are at least 55 years old.

For information: Call 800-456-4000.

COURTYARD BY MARRIOTT

Here AARP or CARP members get 10 percent off the regular room rates every day of the year. Most of these moderately priced hotels feature swimming pools and exercise facilities. Advance reservations are recommended.

For information: Call 800-321-2211.

CROSS COUNTRY INNS

If you check in at one of these inns located in Ohio, Kentucky, and Michigan, you will get a 25 percent discount on your regular room rates every day of the year; but you must belong to AARP, have a Golden Buckeye card, or be over 60.

For information: Call 800-621-1429.

CROWNE PLAZA HOTELS & RESORTS

At participating locations you'll get a minimum of 10 percent off the regular room rates every day of the year simply by showing your AARP card.

For information: Call 800-2 CROWNE (800-227-6963).

DAYS INNS

Join the September Days Club, the lodging industry's first senior travel club, and you'll be entitled to 15 to 50 percent discounts off the standard room rates at all 1,800 Days Inns worldwide. You'll also get a minimum of 10 percent reduction on meals at some locations, plus special rates on car rentals, trips, tours, and local attractions. A quarterly magazine keeps you up to date. Annual membership is $15 for you and your spouse.

If you aren't a member of the club, you'll still get a 10 percent discount on your room rate if you show a membership card from a senior organization such as AARP or CARP. *For information:* Call 800-DAYS-INN (800-329-7466). In Canada, call 800-964-3434. To enroll in September Days Club, call 800-241-5050.

DOUBLETREE HOTELS

All Doubletree Hotels, Doubletree Club Hotels, and Doubletree Guest Suites now give members of AARP an offer that's hard to refuse—if you can make your travel plans early. With a membership card and a 21-day nonrefundable advance booking by credit card, you will get a 40 percent discount on the regular room rates when there is space available. If you can't commit yourself so early, you will still be entitled to 10 percent off the room rates any time, any day, with no advance reservation.

Hotel guests who belong to AARP get something else, too: 10 percent taken off the bill for meals and non-alcoholic beverages at participating Doubletree restaurants. *For information:* Call 800-222-8733.

DOWNTOWNER MOTOR INNS

See Red Carpet Inns. Call 800-251-1962.

DRURY INNS

These economy motels concentrated in the Midwest offer a 10 percent discount on the regular room rates at all of their over 100 locations to anyone 50 or over. Just ask and have your proof of age handy.

For information: Call 800-325-8300.

ECONO LODGES

See Choice Hotels. Some rooms are specially designed for mature travelers. Call 800-55 ECONO (800-553-2666).

ECONOMY INNS OF AMERICA

This economy lodging chain, with 20 motels located near major highways in California and Florida, gives 10 percent off the room rates to anyone over 55. Just ask for it.

For information: Call 800-826-0778.

EMBASSY SUITES

In some of its 140 upscale all-suite hotels, Embassy Suites gives a discount, usually about 10 percent, to travelers over the age of 55. That means you'll have to make inquiries when you make your reservations. Amenities for guests include a complimentary cooked-to-order breakfast every morning and free beverages every evening.

For information: Call 800-EMBASSY (800-362-2779).

FAIRFIELD INN BY MARRIOTT

At Marriott's economy lodging chain, you will get 10 percent deducted from your bill, complimentary continental breakfast, and free local calls if you belong to AARP or CARP or are over 62.

For information: Call 800-228-2800.

FOUR POINTS HOTELS

See Sheraton Hotels & Resorts. Call 800-325-3535.

GRAND HERITAGE HOTELS

This group of upscale inns in the U.S., all restored "grande dame" hotels with historical significance, offers two good deals to guests over 55 or members of a recognized senior organization. The first is a discount of 20 percent off the regular rates any time. The alternative is a 10 percent discount on any published package, promotional, or weekend room rate.

For information: Call 800-HERITAGE (800-437-4824).

HAMPTON INN

The LifeStyle 50 program at this moderately priced group of more than 700 hotels entitles up to four guests to share a room at the one-person rate. All you have to do to get it is to show proof when you check in that one of you has had a 50th birthday.

For information: Call 800-HAMPTON (800-426-7866).

HARLEY HOTELS

Look for a 10 percent discount at 14 Harley properties in the Northeast simply by flashing your AARP or other senior organization card. On weekends, however, the weekend rate may be a better bet.

For information: Call 800-321-2323.

HAWAIIAN HOTELS & RESORTS

At age 55, you'll be eligible for a 30 to 50 percent discount on the regular rates at any of these four hotels which are located on three Hawaiian islands, and sometimes other amenities are offered, such as free breakfast and a discount on car rentals. At two of the hotels, special senior pack-

ages that feature even better deals are also offered.
For information: Call 800-222-5642.

HAWTHORN SUITES HOTELS

AARP members and other guests over 65 get discounts of
30 to 45 percent at this group of suites hotels, most of them
located in the southern states.
For information: Call 800-527-1133.

HILTON HOTELS WORLDWIDE

Hilton's Senior HHonors travel program is a very good deal
for those over the age of 60 who do a lot of traveling. It
gives you up to 50 percent off the regular rates at more than
400 Hilton and Conrad International and Vista Hotels
around the world. Annual membership for you and your
spouse is $50; a lifetime membership currently costs $290.

As a member, you may reserve a second room at the
same reduced rate for family or friends who are traveling
with you and get late checkout privileges when possible.
And you get 20 percent off the bill for dinner for two at
participating hotel restaurants, whether or not you are
guests of the hotel.

For those who don't join the Senior HHonors program
but do belong to AARP, most Hiltons give a discount of 10
to 15 percent.

And, whatever your age, it's wise to sign up for Hilton
HHonors Worldwide, a new guest reward program at
Hiltons all over the world. It gives members both hotel
points and airline frequent-flyer miles for each qualifying
stay. It's free. Join by telephone or at the front desk of a participating hotel.

For information: Call 800-HILTONS (800-445-8667). To enroll in the Hilton Senior HHonors Worldwide, call 800-466-6677.

HOLIDAY INN WORLDWIDE

Holiday Inn Alumni, a travel club for travelers over 50, is a good bet if you spend considerable time on the road because members receive a minimum of 20 percent off the regular room rates at more than one thousand participating hotels worldwide. A continental breakfast for two comes with the room. As a member, you'll also have 10 percent deducted from your food bills at all meals in participating hotel restaurants in North America, whether you're a guest at the hotel or just dropping by for a meal. On your birthday, you'll get a complimentary dinner when another meal is purchased, again whether you're staying at the hotel or not. And, during the Thanksgiving and Christmas holidays, the club rates and benefits are extended to members of your family, too, but you must make the reservations yourself directly with the hotel you choose.

To join Holiday Inn Alumni, call the toll-free number below or sign up at a participating hotel. The first year is free. After that, the membership costs $10 a year, a fee that is waived if you stay a minimum of five nights a year at any Holiday Inn.

All is not lost, however, if you don't join the club because nonmembers over 50 get a 10 percent discount at participating hotels.

For information: Call 800-HOLIDAY (800-465-4329) for reservations. To enroll in the club, call 800-ALUMNI-2 (800-258-6642).

HOWARD JOHNSON INNS & HOTELS

At Howard Johnson's approximately 600 locations in the U.S., Canada, Mexico, and other countries around the world, you are offered a 20 percent discount off the regular rates every day of the year if you belong to AARP. Or your discount is 15 percent if you are over 60 and a member of another national senior organization. Remember to carry your membership card with you because you must present it when you check in.

For information: Call 800-I-GO-HOJO (800-446-4656).

HYATT HOTELS & RESORTS

These upscale hotels in the U.S., Canada, and the Caribbean give guests over the age of 65 a discount of up to 25 percent on the standard room rates. Ask for it. In some international locations, however, the discount goes up to 40 percent, so always check it out when you make your reservations.

For information: Call 800-233-1234.

KIMPTON GROUP HOTELS

All of Kimpton's 21 hotels in cities on the West Coast, most of them in San Francisco, have something good to offer mature travelers. The senior packages at these small, "boutique" hotels, each one different, give you discounts ranging from only a few dollars to more than a third off the regular room rates and often include breakfast, afternoon tea, and evening wine service. You must be a member of AARP or at least 55 in most cases to qualify as a senior.

For information: Call 800-546-2622 and ask for the telephone numbers of the individual hotels.

KNIGHTS INNS

This budget motel chain with more than 200 locations mostly in the East gives a discount of 10 percent every day of the year to members of senior organizations.
For information: Call 800-THE-KNIGHTS (800-843-5644).

LA QUINTA INNS

With over 200 locations in the U.S., these motor inns are inexpensive and become even more so when you ask for your 10 percent discount. You'll get it if you are a member of AARP or a similar organization or if you are 55 and can prove it.
For information: Call 800-531-5900.

LK INNS & LODGEKEEPERS

A budget chain in the Midwest, LK takes 10 percent off for AARP members and anybody else over 55.
For information: Call 800-282-5711.

THE LUXURY COLLECTION

See Sheraton Hotels & Resorts. Call 800-325-3535.

MAINSTAY SUITES

See Choice Hotels. Call 800-660-MAIN (800-660-6246).

MARC RESORTS

If you are at least 55, a 25 percent discount is yours, except during holiday weeks, at Marc Resorts' 20 locations on five Hawaiian islands.
For information: Call 800-535-0085.

MARRIOTT HOTELS, RESORTS & SUITES

Marriott's program for over-50s is among the best deals around if you are a member of AARP or CARP and can plan ahead. With a 21-day nonrefundable advance booking, you will get at least 50 percent off the regular rates at more than 190 participating locations. You must pay in advance for the entire stay by check or credit card when you make your reservation.

For those who can't commit themselves three weeks in the future, there is a flat 10 percent discount on regular room rates every day of the year for AARP or CARP card carriers.

In addition, you are offered a 20 percent discount on food and nonalcoholic beverages at most of the hotels and resorts for your party of up to eight people. This may be used as often as you like, and you are not required to be an overnight guest to get this discount, but you must belong to AARP or CARP. Always ask first if the hotel or resort is participating in the discount plan.

And more: you'll get a 10 percent discount at the gift shops in participating hotels and resorts.

Two hitches: the room discounts may not be available at all times, especially during peak periods, and some Marriotts do not participate in the seniors program.

For information: Call 800-228-9290.

MASTER HOSTS INNS & RESORTS

See Red Carpet Inns. Call 800-251-1962.

MOTEL 6

You can take advantage of a 10 percent discount on the

room rates at these economy motels in more than 755 locations throughout North America if you have an AARP or CARP card.

For information: Call 800-440-6000.

NATIONAL 9 INNS

You'll get a 10 percent discount at age 50 at most of these motels/hotels concentrated in the West.

For information: Call 800-524-9999.

NOVOTEL HOTELS

Each of Novotel's nine midscale hotels in North America has its own senior program, but all of them offer discounts to people of a certain age, in most cases 60.

For information: Call 800-NOVOTEL (800-668-6835).

OMNI HOTELS

Almost all of these upscale hotels—over 40 of them—take 10 percent off the published room rates every day of the week for members of AARP. Cardholders also get a 15 percent discount on food and nonalcoholic beverages in participating restaurants. To get the special room rate, reserve ahead and request the discount. In the restaurants, present your AARP card before you place your order.

For information: Call THE-OMNI (800-843-6664).

ORION APARTMENT HOTELS

More than 50 apartment hotels and resorts in France and other countries in Europe give members of AARP a 10 percent discount on the published rates every day of the year. Advance reservations and deposits are required.

For information: Call 800-987-6650.

OUTRIGGER HOTELS & RESORTS

If you are 50 or older, Outrigger will give you 20 percent off regular published rates at any of its hotels and resorts in Waikiki on Oahu, Maui, Kauai, and the Big Island of Hawaii. You'll have your choice of a suite, an economy kitchenette, or a fully furnished condominium. Not only that, but you also will have the option of a rental car at $25 a day.

For members of AARP or CARP, the room discount is even better—25 percent all year, whenever rooms are available. Proof of age and/or membership are required at check-in.

For information: Call 800-OUTRIGGER (800-688-7444).

PARK INN HOTELS

This group of hotels in the U.S., Europe, and other parts of the world gives a 15 percent discount to members of AARP.

For information: Call 800-437-PARK (800-437-7275).

PASSPORT INNS

See Red Carpet Inns. Call 800-251-1962.

QUALITY INNS

See Choice Hotels. Call 800-228-5151.

RADISSON HOTELS WORLDWIDE

At Radisson's more than 345 locations in 39 countries, take advantage of Senior Breaks, a discount of 25 to 40 percent off the standard rates. The age at which you qualify varies by country—in the U.S. and Canada, it's 50. In Europe, it is usually 65. You'll get the discount year-round, seven days a week, based on space availability. There's no club to join—just carry proof of your age. In addition, most Radissons offer you and your party a discount on dining in hotel restaurants whether or not you are staying at the hotel, except in peak hours.

For information: Call 800-333-3333.

RADISSON SAS HOTELS

The Senior Saver program at these hotels in Europe, Asia, and the Middle East gives everyone over the age of 65 a discount of 25 percent off the normal rates any day of the week when rooms are available.

For information: Call 800-221-2350.

RAMADA CANADA

These hotels across Canada offer a discount to members of AARP and CARP and to other guests over the age of 60. The discount varies from 10 to 25 percent off the standard room rates, depending on the location.

For information: Call 800-854-7854.

RAMADA LIMITED, INNS, AND PLAZA HOTELS

Ramada's Best Years Club, open to anyone at age 60, gives you 25 percent discounts, plus 15 frequent-stayer points for every dollar spent during your stays at more than 750 participating Ramadas. You'll get 3,000 bonus points when you sign up for the club and your accumulated points may be redeemed for free airline tickets, lodging, and travel awards. Other benefits include discounts on travel and car rentals and a quarterly newsletter. Lifetime membership costs $15. To join, sign up at any hotel or call the number below.

Another choice at participating Ramadas when space is available is a 15 percent discount for the over-50 members of AARP or CARP.

For information: Call 800-2 RAMADA (800-272-6232). To enroll in the Best Years Club, call 800-766-2378.

RAMADA INTERNATIONAL HOTELS & RESORTS

At these midscale hotels and resorts, all of them in Europe, if you are 60 years old or belong to any recognized senior organization, you're entitled to the senior rate, a minimum of 25 percent off the regular room rates every day of the year. Ask for it when you make your reservations.

For information: Call 800-854-7854. In Canada, 800-854-7854.

RED CARPET INNS

Virtually all Red Carpet Inns, Passport Inns, Downtowner Motor Inns, and Scottish Inns, about 300 of them in the U.S., the Bahamas, and Jamaica, give a 10 percent discount every day, all year, to members of AARP and anybody else who qualifies as a "senior."

For information: Call 800-251-1962.

RED LION HOTELS & INNS

To everyone over the age of 50, Red Lions—all in the western states—give their Prime Rate, which amounts to 20 percent off the regular room rates. Book ahead, because there are occasional blackout periods. In addition, participating

hotel restaurants give you a 10 percent discount on food and nonalcoholic beverages.
For information: Call 800-547-8010.

RED ROOF INNS

An economy lodging chain with over 250 locations in 33 states, Red Roof offers seniors its RediCard+60 Club. You may join it at 60, paying a lifetime fee of $10 plus $2 for a spouse, and thereafter get a 10 percent discount on room rates. You can sign up at the front desk when you check in or when you call the number below.
For information: Call 800-843-7663.

RENAISSANCE HOTELS & RESORTS

When you make reservations at any of the luxury Renaissance Hotels in the U.S., Mexico, and 22 other countries around the world, ask for the senior rate if you are over 60 or a member of a recognized senior organization. You'll get a minimum of 25 percent off the published room rate any day of the year. Make advance reservations because, as always, rooms at special rates are limited.
For information: Call 800-228-9898.

RESIDENCE INN BY MARRIOTT

These extended-stay all-suite accommodations complete with kitchens offer members of AARP or CARP a 15 percent discount on regular rates every day of the year when space is available. Complimentary continental breakfast, weekday social hours, and weekly barbecues are included.
For information: Call 800-331-3131.

RODEWAY INNS

See Choice Hotels. And check out Rodeway's new "senior-friendly" rooms, which feature such amenities as bright lighting and big TV control buttons. Call 800-228-3323.

SANDMAN HOTELS

All situated in western Canada, these 20 inns take 20 percent off the regular room rate if you are 55 or over. Show proof of age at check-in or, better yet, call the number below and ask for a Club 55 Card. It's free.
For information: Call 800-726-3626.

SCOTTISH INNS

See Red Carpet Inns. Call 800-251-1962.

SHERATON HOTELS & RESORTS

All Sheratons around the world give you a break if you are over 60 or a member of AARP, CARP, or a long list of other recognized senior organizations, and are traveling for pleasure not business. That's 15 to 25 percent off the published room rates. You may also reserve another room for family members at the senior rate when you are traveling together. Sometimes, however, these hotels have special sales going on that are better than the senior rate, so always ask for the best available price at the hotel you plan to visit. Affiliated hotels—The Luxury Collection and Four Points Hotels—give seniors the same discount at all of their locations.

As for the seven resort hotels in Hawaii, these offer a discount of 25 percent on regular rates to AARP members and all others over 55.
For information: Call 800-325-3535.

SHONEY'S INNS

Economy lodgings, Shoney's approximately 85 locations scattered throughout the southeastern states take 15 percent off the room rates for members of AARP any time, any day of the week. If you are not a member but are at least 55 years old, you will get a 10 percent discount when rooms are available.

For information: Call 800-222-2222.

SLEEP INNS

See Choice Hotels. Call 800-SLEEP INN (800-753-3746).

SONESTA INTERNATIONAL HOTELS

This collection of upscale hotels in the U.S., Egypt, and the Caribbean gives members of AARP a 15 percent discount off the regular rates. You must make reservations in advance, of course.

For information: Call 800-SONESTA (800-766-3782).

SUPER 8 MOTELS

Almost all of these over 1,600 no-frills economy motels in the U.S. and Canada give a 10 percent discount to members of AARP.

For information: Call 800-800-8000.

SUSSE CHALETS

At these motels and inns scattered around the Northeast, you will get a room for up to four people for the price of a single room. You must be 60 or older to qualify.

For information: Call 800-5-CHALET (800-524-2538).

DISNEY DISCOUNTS

If you're a Disney theme parks fan and over 55, inquire about a Magic Kingdom Club Gold Card. For a $50 two-year membership ($15 less than regular membership price), you and your immediate family get reduced ticket prices to theme parks worldwide and reductions at many Disney restaurants and resort hotels—plus savings on car rentals, new AAA memberships, and merchandise. Members are kept up to date on news and events by a magazine and a newsletter. *For information:* Call 800-56-DISNEY (800-563-4763).

TRAVELODGES HOTELS & MOTELS

All Travelodges and Thriftlodges, more than 500 of them throughout North and South America, have a nice straightforward plan for older travelers. This is a simple unrestricted 15 percent discount off the room rates any time, any night, for members of AARP and CARP with advance reservations through the toll-free number and 10 percent to anybody over 50 without reservations when rooms are available.

For information: Call 800-578-7878.

VAGABOND INNS

Vagabond's Smart Senior Program is one of the better deals around. It gives you 30 percent off the standard rates at age 55 at all except one of these economy inns on the West Coast. This group of hotels also has its Vagabuck Program, which gives you $5 in play money every time you check out. Use it the next time you stay at a Vagabond Inn.

For Information: Call 800-522-1555.

VILLAGER LODGES

At most of these economy extended-stay motels, you can get a room with a kitchenette at a discount of 10 percent off the daily rate if you belong to AARP or are over the age of 60.

For information: Call 800-328-7829.

WELLESLEY INNS

This group of inns located on the East Coast, mostly in Florida, gives members of AARP a discount of 10 percent off the regular room rates. Sometimes, however, there are special offers, so ask about them. Complimentary continental breakfast is included.

For information: Call 800-444-8888.

WESTCOAST HOTELS

If you are over 55, ask for the senior rate at these 26 mid-scale and grand hotels in the western states and Hawaii. The discount varies by location.

For information: Call 800-426-0670.

WESTIN HOTELS & RESORTS

Many of these luxury hotels offer senior rates but each has its own policy, so always ask about the possibilities when you make reservations. And if you are a member of United Silver Wings Plus, you will get your room at 50 percent off the published rate at participating hotels.

For information: Call 800-228-3000.

WINGATE INNS

A hotel chain with midscale prices for rooms with high-tech amenities, Wingate Inns gives a 15 percent discount off published room rates to members of a large number of senior organizations.

For information: Call 800-228-1000.

WYNDHAM HOTELS & RESORTS

Wyndham's offer to guests over 60 is a discount of 20 percent on the weekday corporate rates and weekend rates at its properties in the U.S. and Canada. At its resorts in the Caribbean, guests 60 and over get 50 percent off the standard rates—except at the all-inclusive resorts, where the discount is 25 percent.

For information: Call 800-WYNDHAM (800-996-3426).

GOOD DEALS IN RESTAURANTS

Many restaurants offer special deals to people in their prime, but in most cases you must seek them out yourself by reading the menu, asking at the restaurant, or watching the ads in the local newspapers. At some big chains, such as the International House of Pancakes, Kentucky Fried Chicken, Applebee's, and Wendy's, there's a recommended corporate policy of senior discounts or special senior menus that may or may not be followed at its franchised restaurants.

Sometimes a senior discount is available any time you decide to dine, but often it's good only during certain hours or as "early bird" specials before 5 or 6 P.M. The eligible age varies from 55 to 65, and occasionally a restaurant requires that you sign up for its free senior club that issues you a membership card.

In addition, a few hotel chains will give you a break on your meal checks when you eat in their restaurants. For example:

At participating **Hilton Hotels** restaurants in the U.S. and

Canada, you're entitled to a 20 percent discount on dinners for two, hotel guests or not, if one of you is a member of Hilton's Senior HHonors Worldwide.

Holiday Inn restaurants give a discount of 10 percent off your check when you dine there, whether or not you are a guest at the inn, if you belong to the Holiday Inn Alumni, a travel club for over-50s. On your birthday, your dinner is free when another meal is purchased.

The restaurants in the participating **Marriott Hotels and Resorts** will take 20 percent off your bill, except on alcoholic beverages, for a party of up to eight people if you belong to AARP or CARP, whether or not you are guests of the hotel.

If you join the September Days Club, you'll get room discounts at **Days Inns** worldwide and also a minimum of 10 percent off meals at participating locations.

Doubletree Hotels take 10 percent off the bill for food and nonalcoholic beverages in participating restaurants for members of AARP who are guests at the hotel.

At most **Omni Hotels** you'll get 15 percent taken off the check for food and nonalcoholic beverages in the hotel restaurants by flashing your AARP card.

You'll get a reduction of 15 percent on your food bills for yourself and your party when you eat at participating **Radisson Hotels Worldwide** restaurants, whether or not you are hotel guests. You qualify for the savings at age 50 in U.S. locations and usually at 65 in Europe.

Many of the restaurants at **Red Lion Inns** will reduce your bill by 10 percent on food chosen from the regular menu, except on holidays, if you are over 50.

11

Alternative Lodgings for Thrifty Wanderers

If you're willing to be innovative, imaginative, and occasionally fairly spartan, you can travel for a song or thereabouts. Here are some novel kinds of lodgings that can save you money and perhaps offer adventures in the bargain. Not all of them are designed specifically for people over 50, but each reports that the major portion of its clientele consists of free spirits of a certain age who like to travel, appreciate good values for their money, and enjoy meeting new people from other places.

For more ways to cut travel costs and get smart at the same time, check out the residential/educational programs in Chapter 16.

AFFORDABLE TRAVEL CLUB

Join this bed-and-breakfast club for mature travelers and you'll pay a pittance for accommodations, meet interesting people, and see new places. You may join as a host member, putting up other travelers in your spare bedroom a couple of times a year and providing breakfast and a little of your time to acquaint your guests with your area. Visitors pay $15 for a single or $20 for a double per night for their stay. In return, you get to stay in other people's homes for the same token fee when you travel. Or you may prefer to be a nonhost member, using the guest privileges only and paying $25 for a single or $30 for a double per night.

There are currently about a thousand members in this club in 45 states and 25 countries offering accommodations ranging from simple bedrooms to suites and condos. The annual host membership fee per household is $50, while a nonhost membership costs $90 a year. It entitles you to a quarterly newsletter and a directory that lists and describes the host homes. The club also sponsors a group tour at least once a year.

If you have a pet, you may want to take advantage of the club's house-sitting and pet-sitting service—members move into your house and care for your house and/or pets while you're on vacation, meanwhile enjoying a visit to your neighborhood in exchange.

For information: Affordable Travel Club, 6556 Snug Harbor Ln., Gig Harbor, WA 98335; 253-858-2172.

AMERICAN-INTERNATIONAL HOMESTAYS

Travel to a foreign land and stay in the homes of local residents. Immerse yourself in the country's customs and traditions, with your English-speaking hosts acting as your personal guides and interpreters. You'll have your own bedroom in the hosts' home and become part of the family, eat-

ing meals and exploring your surroundings together. An inexpensive way to travel, homestays provide a unique way to experience other cultures. AIH handles all the travel arrangements for individuals or groups for stays all over the world, from Australia, Belgium, China, Ecuador, Germany, India, Lithuania, and Japan to Mongolia, Ukraine, Uzbekistan, and the Kyrgyz Republic.

For information: American-International Homestays, PO Box 1754, Nederland, CO 80466; 800-876-2048 or 303-642-3088.

COOPER COMMUNITIES

This group of five retirement villages located in Arkansas, Tennessee, South Carolina, and Missouri tempts potential residents to visit its planned communities by offering them inexpensive Get Acquainted lodging packages. If you want to sample one of the villages, you may stay for very little if you agree to take a sales tour around the property. Depending on the location, lodging rates range from $29 for two nights to $60 per night.

At most of the communities, the amenities include golf courses, tennis courts, hiking trails, boating, and recreation centers, all of which guests are invited to use.

For information: Cooper Communities, 800-228-7328.

DEL WEBB'S SUN CITIES

Seven Sun Cities operated by the Del Webb Corporation offer Vacation Getaway programs designed as sample stays, just in case you're thinking of moving to one of these active adult communities. It's a way to experience the lifestyle and explore the neighborhood to see if it suits you. For remarkably little, you'll have your own villa for three, four,

or seven nights starting any day of the week and enjoy all the facilities: tennis, golf, swimming, aerobics, massages, and socializing with residents and staff. Depending on the season and the location, the rates range from about $179 for three nights all year to about $575 for a seven-day package in the high season.

The only requirements are that one partner in a visiting couple is at least 55 years old and no one in your party is under 19.

The communities currently offering Vacation Getaways include Sun City Grand in Phoenix, Sun City MacDonald Ranch and Sun City Summerlin in Las Vegas, Sun City Palm Desert in Palm Springs, Sun City Roseville in Sacramento, Sun City Hilton Head, and Sun City Georgetown in Austin, Texas.

For information: Sun Cities, 6001 N. 24th St., Phoenix, AZ 85016; 800-4-DEL WEBB (800-433-5932).

ELDERHOSTEL HOMESTAYS

Elderhostel collaborates with World Learning, a 65-year-old institution specializing in international education and homestays, to place hostelers in the homes of local families in Europe, Asia, Mexico, and New Zealand. The homestay programs—two to three weeks long—begin with a week of lectures, classes, and field trips to introduce you to the local history and culture. Then you move into your host home to spend a few days as a member of the family. Those participating in three-week programs meet for an additional week of classes and excursions before heading home.

For information: Elderhostel, Dept. M2, PO Box 1959, Wakefield, MA 01880; 617-426-7788.

EVERGREEN BED & BREAKFAST CLUB

This is a bed-and-breakfast club for singles or couples over 50 who accommodate one another in their own homes. Members receive an annual directory that lists pertinent information about each host and the special attractions of the area. Arrangements are made directly with the hosts. Whether a home is elegant or simple, the cost is only a modest gratuity paid directly to the host. Members may choose not to entertain guests, but many do. Those who do serve as hosts themselves pay $10 per day single, $15 per day double, to stay at the homes of other members. Those who prefer not to be hosts pay a little more per day, $18 for one or $24 for two.

The club currently has about 2,000 members, with 900 host locations in the United States and Canada and a few in Mexico and Europe. Annual club dues are $40 single and $50 double.

For information: Evergreen Club, PO Box 1430, Falls Church, VA 22041; 800-EVERGREEN (800-383-7473).

NEW PALTZ SUMMER LIVING

Think about spending a couple of the hottest months in the mountains, about 75 miles north of New York City. Every summer, while the usual student occupants are on vacation, 140 furnished garden apartments are reserved for seniors in the village of New Paltz, near Mohonk Mountain and home of a branch of the State University of New York. The rents at this writing for the entire summer (from early June until late August) range from $1,325 to $3,600, depending on the size of the apartment. Living right in town next to the campus, you may audit college courses free, attend lectures and cultural events, and take part in planned activities in the clubhouse. There is a heated pool and a tennis court in the complex. Buses travel to New York frequently for those who want to go to the theater, and there are frequent day trips to places of interest.

For information: New Paltz Summer Living, 19 E. Colonial Dr., New Paltz, NY 12561; 800-431-4143 or 914-255-7205.

RETREAT CENTER GUEST HOUSES
If you are seeking a refuge from the pressures of daily life and time for quiet reflection, a stay at a retreat center may be your answer. Retreat centers are church-affiliated compounds where guests of any religious preference (or none at all) and of any age may find lodging and three meals for $35 to $45 a day. *Retreat Center Guest House Guide* describes more than 850 such centers in the U.S., Canada, Europe, New Zealand, and Australia.

For information: CTS Publications, PO Box 8355, Newport Beach, CA 92660; 714-720-3729.

ROYAL COURT APARTMENTS
As an alternative to hotels, one-, two-, and three-bedroom apartments are available all year at the Royal Court in central London, one block from Hyde Park, giving you plenty of space and a home at the end of a busy day. You'll get a discount of 10 percent if you are over 50 and mention this book when you make your reservations.

For information: Royal Court Apartments, British Network Ltd., 594 Valley Rd., Upper Montclair, NJ 07043; 800-274-8583 or 201-744-5215.

SENIORS ABROAD

Seniors Abroad arranges for Americans to spend time—three weeks in Japan or four weeks in Australia and New Zealand—staying with families abroad and learning about their lives and cultures. If you go, you'll stay for five days or a week in each of three to five homes in different parts of the country you're visiting. Your hosts are your tour guides, treating you as members of the family and introducing you to their communities and the sights around them. You may also host visitors from foreign countries in your own home. All hospitality is voluntary on the part of the hosts and without cost to the guests, except for travel, tours, and hotel stays.

For information: Seniors Abroad, 12533 Pacato Circle North, San Diego, CA 92128; 619-485-1696.

SERVAS

Servas is an international cooperative system of hosts and travelers established to help promote world peace, goodwill, and understanding among peoples. A nonprofit, nongovernmental, interracial, and interfaith organization open to all ages, it provides approved travelers with a list of hosts—14,000 in all—in 137 countries, including the U.S. To participate, you make your own arrangements to visit hosts, usually for two days at a time, in their homes. No money changes hands. The hospitable people, all peace activists, who offer to share their space with you are eager to learn about you and your culture. You may do the same for other travelers in return, if you wish.

Travelers must pay a membership fee of $55 per year and are asked for two letters of reference and an interview.

Hosts are interviewed and asked for a voluntary donation of $25 or more per year.

For information: Send a #10 self-addressed, stamped envelope to US Servas, 11 John St., Room 407, New York, NY 10038; 212-267-0252.

SUN CITY CENTER

Between Tampa and Sarasota, Florida, Sun City Center wants you to discover what a large, self-contained retirement town is all about and offers an inexpensive vacation package so you can sample the life there. You may stay for a few days or more. At this writing, a stay of four days/three nights with daily continental breakfast, tennis, swimming, and club facilities costs $99 per couple from April 15 through January 15 and $189 from January 16 through April 14. A round of golf costs extra, but this is the home of the Ben Sutton School of Golf and offers 126 holes. The only hitch: you must take a tour of the town accompanied by a salesperson.

For information: Sun City Center, PO Box 5698, Sun City Center, FL 33571; 800-237-8200.

12

Perks in Parks and Other Good News

Here and there throughout the United States and Canada, enterprising officials in states, provinces, and cities have initiated some enticing programs designed to capture the imagination of the mature population. Often they are expressing their appreciation of our many contributions to society and simply want to do something nice for us. And sometimes they are trying to attract us and our vacation dollars to their vicinity, having discovered that we're always eager to enjoy ourselves and know a good deal when we see one.

But, first, keep in mind:

■ Before you set off for a new place, it's a good idea to write ahead for free maps, calendars of events, booklets describing sites and scenes of interest, accommodation guides, and perhaps even a list of special discounts or other good things that are available to you as a person over 50.

■ Many states offer passes to their state parks and recreation facilities free or at reduced prices to people who are old enough to have learned how to treat those areas respectfully.

■ After the section on national parks, you'll find information about state park passes and special events in many states. There may be other good deals that have escaped our attention, but those in this chapter are probably the cream of the crop.

ESCAPEES CLUB

Escapees is a club dedicated to providing a support network for RVers, full-time or part-time, most of whom are on the far side of 50. It publishes a bimonthly magazine filled with useful information for travelers who carry their homes with them, organizes rallies in the U.S., Canada, and Mexico, and hosts five-day seminars on RV living. Other benefits include discounted co-op RV parks and campgrounds, emergency road service, mail service, and voice message service. After a $10 fee to join, the annual membership fee is $50 a year.

The club has recently established its own CARE Center (Continuing Assistance for Retired Escapees), a separate RV campground where retired members can live independently in their own RVs while receiving medical and living assistance, housekeeping, and transportation services as needed.
For information: Escapees Inc., 100 Rainbow Drive, Livingston, TX 77351; 888-757-2582 or 409-327-8873.

NATIONAL PARKS

GOLDEN AGE PASSPORT

Available for $10 to anyone over 62, this lifetime pass admits you free of charge to all of the federal government's parks, forests, refuges, monuments, and recreation areas that charge entrance fees. Anybody who accompanies you in the same car or RV also gets in free. If you turn up at the gate in a commercial vehicle such as a van or bus, the passport admits you and your spouse, your children, and even your parents, so remember to take them along.

You will also get a 50 percent discount on federal use fees charged for facilities and services such as camping, boat launching, parking, or cave tours.

The passport is not available by mail. You must pick one up in person at any National Park System area where entrance fees are charged or at any offices of the National Park Service, the U.S. Forest Service, the Fish and Wildlife Service, or the Bureau of Land Management. You must have proof of age. A driver's license will do just fine.

(The free Golden Access Passport provides the same benefits for the disabled of any age. The Golden Eagle Passport, for those under 62, costs $25 per year.)

For information: National Park Service, PO Box 37127, Washington, DC 20013.

CANADIAN NATIONAL PARKS

The national parks and national historic sites throughout Canada charge modest entry fees for adults and take 25 percent off those for seniors. The same is generally true for provincial parks.

OFFERINGS FROM THE STATES

Virtually every state has a special senior rate for hunting and fishing licenses for people over a certain age (usually 65). Some states require no license at all for seniors, while others give you a reduced fee (usually half). Most require that you are a resident of the state to get these privileges. Most states also offer state park discounts to seniors, usually only residents, reducing or eliminating entrance fees and marking down camping rates. To check out the regulations in your state or a state you are visiting, call the state or local parks department or the state tourism office.

For a free listing of all the state tourism offices and their toll-free numbers, send a self-addressed, stamped envelope to Discover America, Travel Industry Association of America, 1100 New York Ave. NW, Ste. 450, Washington, DC 20005-3934.

CALIFORNIA

Campers 62 or over get $2 taken off admissions and overnight camping fees in all state parks. Just show your ID at the gate.

For information: Call 800-444-7275 for making campsite reservations.

If you are going to visit Long Beach, call ahead for the *Senior Saver Getaway Guide*. It lists the senior discounts at some of this city's hotels and attractions.

For information: Long Beach Area Convention and Visitors Bureau, 1 World Trade Center, Long Beach, CA 90831; 800-452-7829.

Carmel on the Monterey Peninsula also has some literature for you. It offers *Carmel's Escape for Seniors*, a free brochure describing a few discounts for people over the age of 55 at galleries, theaters, restaurants, shops, and accommodations. The catch: the discounts are not valid on Fridays or Saturdays or any time during July or August.

For information: Carmel Business Assn., PO Box 4444, Carmel, CA 93921; 800-550-4333 or 408-624-2522.

COLORADO

The Aspen Leaf Pass entitles Colorado residents 62 and over to free entrance to state parks any day and camping Sundays through Thursdays. The pass costs $10 per year.

For information: Colorado Division of State Parks, 1313 Sherman St., Room 618, Denver CO 80203; 303-866-3437.

CONNECTICUT

Residents of Connecticut who are over 65 get a free lifetime Charter Oak Pass that gets them into state parks and forests plus Gillette Castle, Dinosaur Park, and Quinebaug Valley Hatchery for free. To get your pass, write to the address below and send along a copy of your current Connecticut driver's license.

For information: DEP, Charter Oak Pass, State Parks Division, DEP, 79 Elm St., Hartford, CT 06106-5127; 860-424-3200.

INDIANA

The Golden Hoosier Passport admits Indiana residents over the age of 60 and fellow passengers in a private vehicle to all state parks and natural resources without charge. An application for the Passport, which costs $5 a year, is available at all state parks or from the Indiana State Parks Department.

For information: Indiana State Parks Dept., 402 W. Washington St., Room W298, Indianapolis, IN 46204; 317-232-4124.

MAINE

Pick up your free Senior Citizen Pass and you will pay no day-use fees at Maine state parks and historic sites. The pass is available at any state park or by writing to the Bureau of Parks and Lands and including proof of your age.

For information: Maine Bureau of Parks and Lands, State House Station 22, Augusta, ME 04333; 207-287-3821.

MICHIGAN

You can get some good deals in Michigan if you are a resident who's reached the age of 65. These include a motor-vehicle permit that gets you into all state parks for $5 a year, a fishing license with an annual fee of $1 a year, and a hunting license that costs $4 a year.

For information: Call the Department of Natural Resources at 517-373-9900.

MISSOURI

Missouri residents over the age of 60 are entitled to a free Silver Citizen Discount Card that gives them discounts at restaurants, stores, services, pharmacies, and other businesses throughout the state. To get a card, call the toll-free number below.

For information: Missouri Dept. of Social Services, PO Box 1337, Jefferson City, MO 65102-1337; 800-235-5503.

MONTANA

You need pay only half the usual camping fee in Montana's state parks if you are over the age of 62.
For information: Montana Fish, Wildlife, and Parks Dept., 1420 E. 6th Ave., Helena, MT 59620; 406-444-4041.

NEW HAMPSHIRE

Seniors Week at Mt. Washington Valley, in the White Mountains of New Hampshire, takes place every September just after Labor Day. Here, in the villages of Eaton, Conway, Pinkham Notch, North Conway, Bartlett, Glen, Madison, and Jackson, in this spectacularly beautiful high country, everyone over the age of 55 is entitled to discounted lodging prices, restaurant specials, retail discounts, and an array of events and activities.
For information: Mt. Washington Valley Visitors Bureau, PO Box 2300, North Conway, NH 03860; 800-367-3364 or 603-356-3171.

NEVADA

In Carson City, you will strike silver without doing any digging—if you are over 50 and join the free Seniors Strike Silver Club. You'll get a list of discounts in town, plus a membership card to present as identification to participating merchants.
For information: Carson City Convention & Visitors Bureau, 1900 S. Carson St., Carson City, NV 89701; 800-NEVADA 1 (800-638-2321).

NEW MEXICO

For a brochure listing senior discounts at attractions, stores, hotels, restaurants, and transportation in Albuquerque, call the toll-free number below.

For information: Albuquerque Convention & Visitors Bureau; 800-284-2282.

NEW YORK

Simply by presenting your current valid New York driver's license or a New York nondriver's identification card, you will be entitled to all of the privileges of the Golden Park Program for residents over the age of 62. The program offers, any weekday except holidays, free vehicle access to state parks and arboretums, free entrance to state historic sites, and reduced fees for state-operated swimming, golf, tennis, and boat rentals. Just show your driver's license or ID card to the guard at each facility as you enter.

For information: State Parks, Albany, NY 12238; 518-474-0456.

OHIO

Residents of Ohio who are 60 or over may apply for a free Golden Buckeye Card, which entitles them to discounts, typically about 10 percent, on goods and services at thousands of participating businesses throughout the state. Applications are available at local sign-up sites. For a list of merchants in the program, call the number below.

For information and the sign-up site nearest your home: Golden Buckeye Unit, Ohio Dept. of Aging, 50 W. Broad St., 9th floor, Columbus, OH 43215; 800-422-1976 or 614-466-3681.

PENNSYLVANIA

Send for a free brochure called *Philadelphia Mature Travelers Discounts* for a list of discounts available in this historic city. It lists dozens of Philadelphia sites and attractions, restaurants, hotels, tours, museums, stores, and cultural events that offer special discounts for visitors over 50.

More good news for seniors in Philadelphia, whether visitors or residents, is the free transportation offered by SEPTA, the regional railway, bus, trolley, and subway system. If you are over 65 and have a Medicare, Railroad Retirement Annuity, or Senior Citizen Transit Identification card, you may ride free weekdays from 9 A.M. to 3:30 P.M., 6:30 P.M. to 6 A.M., and all day weekends and holidays. On the regional rail lines, you ride free or at reduced rates on all off-peak trains if you have the proper ID card.

For information: Philadelphia Visitors Center, 16th Street and JFK Blvd., Philadelphia, PA 19102; 800-537-7676. For information about SEPTA, call 215-580-7800.

SOUTH CAROLINA

Residents of South Carolina who are 65 or older must merely show their driver's licenses to get free admission at all state parks, plus half off on both the camping fees at all parks and the greens fees at Hickory Knob and Cheraw State Parks.

For information: South Carolina Department of Parks, Recreation, and Tourism, 1205 Pendleton St., Columbia, SC 29201; 803-734-0166.

TENNESSEE

Anyone over the age of 62, state resident or not, gets a 10

percent discount on food at park restaurants, cabins, and rooms at the Resort Park Inns. Tennessee residents over 62 are charged only 50 percent of the regular camping fees, while out-of-state campers are entitled to a 25 percent reduction. Admission to all state parks is free, regardless of your age.

For information: Tennessee State Parks, 401 Church St., LC Tower, Nashville, TN 37243; 800-421-6683.

UTAH

The Silver Card issued by Park City, an old mining town known for its great ski mountains, is a free summer program of discounts that gives you 10 percent or more off on merchandise, tickets, and meals. Pick up your card and an information packet for seniors at a participating hotel or the Park City Visitors Bureau.

For information: Park City Convention and Visitors Bureau, 1910 Prospector Ave., Park City, UT 84060; 800-453-1360 or 801-649-6100.

VERMONT

Vermont's residents over 60 may purchase a Green Mountain Passport for $2 from their own town clerk. It is good for a lifetime and entitles them to free or reduced day-use admission at any Vermont State Park and its programs. Other benefits include discounts on concerts, restaurant meals, prescriptions, and more.

For information: Vermont Dept. of Aging, 103 S. Main St., Waterbury, VT 05676; 802-241-2400.

GOOD SAM CLUB

The **Good Sam Club** is an international organization of people who travel in recreational vehicles, mentioned here because the vast majority of those in rolling homes are over 50. Its goal is to make RVing safer, more enjoyable, and less expensive. Among the benefits are 10 percent discounts on nightly fees at over two thousand RV parks and campgrounds, plus more discounts on propane, parts, and accessories at hundreds of service centers.

The club offers a toll-free hotline, a lost-key service, lost-pet service, trip routing, mail forwarding, telephone message service, insurance, a magazine, and campground directories. Most important, it provides low-cost emergency road service anywhere in the U.S. and Canada, including Alaska. Social activities include Good Sam rallies and travel tours and cruises all over the world. And about 2,100 local chapters in the U.S. and Canada hold campouts and meetings and participate in local volunteer projects. Membership is $25 a year per family, $44 for two years.

For information: The Good Sam Club, PO Box 6903, Englewood, CO 80155; 800-234-3450.

VIRGINIA

In this state that abounds with historical sites, you'll find senior discounts almost everywhere you go. You'll get them, for example, at Colonial Williamsburg, Busch Gardens, Berkeley Plantation, Mount Vernon, Woodlawn Plantation, Gunston Hall Plantation, the Edgar Allan Poe Museum in Richmond, and the Virginia Air and Space Center.

For information: Virginia Division of Tourism, 1021 E. Cary St., Richmond, VA 23219; 800-786-4484.

WASHINGTON, D.C.

The Golden Washingtonian Club is a discount program in the nation's capital for people over 55. With proof of age, both residents and visitors may get discounts from about 1,700 merchants listed in the *Gold Mine Directory*, free at many hotels or at the Washington Visitor Information Center. More than 30 hotels offer 10 to 40 percent off regular rates, many restaurants take a percentage off meals, and many retail stores do the same for purchases.

For information: Family and Child Services of Washington, D.C., 929 L St. NW, Washington, DC 20001; 202-289-1510, ext. 186.

WEST VIRGINIA

Everybody who turns 60 in West Virginia gets a Golden Mountaineer Discount Card, which entitles the bearer to discounts from more than 3,500 participating merchants and professionals in the state and a few outside of it. If you don't receive a card from the state soon after your 60th birthday, you may apply for one at your local senior center or by calling the number below. Flash it wherever you go and save a few dollars.

For information: West Virginia Bureau of Senior Services, 1900 Kanawha Blvd. East, Charleston, WV 25305; 304-558-3317.

13

Good Deals for Good Sports

Real sports never give up their sneakers. If you've been a physically active person all your life, you're certainly not going to become a couch potato now—especially since you've probably got more time, energy, and maybe funds, than you ever had before to enjoy athletic activities. Besides, you can now take advantage of some interesting special privileges and adventures offered exclusively to people over 49.

The choices described here are not for those whose interest in sports is limited to watching football games on television or sitting on hard benches in stadiums with cans of beer. They are for energetic people who do the running themselves.

AMERICAN WILDERNESS EXPERIENCE
Action vacations are the specialty of AWE (see Chapter 3),

an agency that offers trips from a great many tour operators. You may choose from a long list of adventures ranging from horseback trips to sailing, canoeing, kayaking, hiking, trekking, dog sledding, scuba diving, biking, cross-country skiing, and other vigorous options, some of them specifically for people over 50.

For information: American Wilderness Experience, Inc., PO Box 1486, Boulder, CO 80306; 800-444-0099 or 303-444-2622.

ELDERCAMP AT CANYON RANCH

ElderCamp is a seven-night health and fitness program for over-60s, offered at least once a year at Canyon Ranch, an upscale fitness resort in Tucson. The purpose is to help you make positive changes in your lifestyle for "healthy aging." A combination of education and exercise, the program includes daily aerobics and stretching; morning walks; sports; sessions with physicians, nutritionists, and therapists; relaxation instruction; group sessions on relevant issues; medical evaluations; and three healthy meals a day. Financial assistance is available for a limited number of participants for any of the spa's life-enhancement wellness weeks, this one included.

For information: Canyon Ranch, 8600 E. Rockcliff Rd., Tucson, AZ 85750; 800-726-9900.

ELDERHOSTEL SPORTS PROGRAMS

More and more Elderhostel programs (see Chapter 16) now include an active sport among their three courses for a residential academic week. For example, the University of Calgary offers hiking in the Rockies, sea kayaking, and bicycling; Bethel Historical Society/Sunday River in Maine includes hiking in western Maine, canoeing, and biking. Others present classes in cross-country skiing, downhill skiing, snowshoeing, and trail biking. Some programs focus exclusively on outdoor pursuits, such as The Outdoor Lodge in Glen Sutton, Quebec, which provides instruction in golf, biking, day walking, hiking, or tennis, and Yavapai College in Arizona, where you'll spend five days on a mountain bike tour visiting the Grand Canyon and Pipe Springs National Monument.

For information: Elderhostel, 75 Federal St., Boston, MA 02110; 617-426-7788. In Canada: Elderhostel Canada, 5 Cataraqui St., Kingston, ON K7K 1Z7; 613-530-2222.

OUTDOOR VACATIONS FOR WOMEN OVER 40

Check out the offerings of this unusual agency specializing in vacations for women who love the outdoors and like to hike, bike, camp, ski, raft, and canoe with contemporaries. Trips are from five days to two weeks long, with accommodations ranging from charming country inns, rustic lodges, and chateaus to windjammer bunks or sleeping bags under the sky.

Current adventures include barging and biking in Holland, hiking and rafting in the Tetons and Yellowstone, walking in Ireland and Tuscany, hiking in the Canadian Rockies, and going on safari in Kenya and Tanzania.

For information: Outdoor Vacations for Women Over 40, PO Box 200, Groton, MA 01450; 978-448-3331.

THE OVER THE HILL GANG

This is a club that welcomes fun-loving, adventurous,

peppy people over 50 (and younger spouses) who are looking for action and contemporaries to pursue it with. No
naps, no rockers, no sitting by the pool sipping planter's
punch. The Over the Hill Gang started as a ski club many
years ago but its members can now be found participating
in all kinds of activities. Recent trips have included skiing
at Keystone, Taos, Steamboat, Vail, Big Sky, and other ski
areas in the West, Val d'Isere in France, Valle Nevado in
Chile, and in New Zealand. Plus whitewater rafting in
Idaho, biking on Cape Cod and in Hawaii, rafting in the
Grand Canyon, golfing in the Canadian Rockies.

The club currently has about 5,500 members in 50
states and 14 countries and 11 regional Gangs (chapters).
Each local Gang decides on its own activities. If there's no
chapter in your vicinity, you may become a member-at-large
and participate in any of the activities.

The annual membership fee ($40 single, $65 for a couple) brings you a quarterly magazine, discounts, information about national and chapter events, and a chance to join
the fun. The local Gangs charge small additional yearly
dues.

For information: Over the Hill Gang International, 3310
Cedar Heights Dr., Colorado Springs, CO 80904; 719-685-
4656.

ADVENTURES FOR BIKERS

Biking has become one of America's most popular sports,
and people who never dreamed they could go much farther than around the block are now pedaling up to 50

miles in a day. That includes over-the-hill bikers as well as youngsters of 16, 39, or 49. In fact, some tours and clubs are designated specifically for over-50s.

THE CROSS CANADA CYCLE TOUR SOCIETY

This is a bicycling club for retired people who love to jump on their bikes and take off across the countryside. Most of the club's members are over 60, with many in their 70s and 80s and only a few under 50. Says the society, "Our aim is to stay alive as long as possible." Now there's a worthwhile goal.

Based in Vancouver, B.C., with members—both men and women, skilled and novice—mostly in B.C., Ontario, and Alberta, it organizes many trips a year, all led by volunteer tour guides. Membership costs $25 single or $35 per couple and includes a monthly newsletter to keep you up to date on happenings. Several times a week, local members gather for day rides, and several times a year there are longer club trips to such far-ranging locations as the San Juan Islands, Waterton Park in Canada, and Glacier National Park in the U.S., Australia, Hawaii's Big Island, Arizona, New Zealand, and Denmark. Every few years a group of intrepid bikers pedals clear across Canada, an adventure that takes a few weeks to accomplish, with some members dropping in and out along the way. Many of the longer trips are tenting or camping tours, while others put you up in hostels, motels, or hotels.

For information: Cross Canada Cycle Tour Society, 6943 Antrim Ave., Burnaby, BC V5J 4M5; 604-433-7710.

ELDERHOSTEL BICYCLE TOURS

Elderhostel's famous educational travel programs include both domestic and foreign bicycle tours among its many offerings. These vary by the season and the year and are all listed in the organization's frequent and voluminous catalogs. Recent tours in the U.S. have included six-day inn-to-inn pedals along the Erie Canal in New York State, the northwest corner of Arizona, and the rolling hills of Texas. Lectures and sight-seeing are included.

Bike tours in foreign lands are scheduled weekly from April through September in Bermuda, England's East Anglia, the coastal islands of Denmark, along the Danube in Austria, the chateaux country of France, and the villages of the Netherlands. You cover 25 to 35 miles a day and learn about the culture and history from local guest lecturers. Three-speed bikes are provided, as are breakfast and dinner and accommodations in small hotels. The support van that travels with the group to carry the luggage and repair equipment will carry you too if you decide you can't possibly make it up another hill.

For information: Elderhostel, 75 Federal St., Boston, MA 02110; 617-426-7788. In Canada: Elderhostel Canada, 5 Cataraqui St., Kingston ON K7K 1Z7; 613-530-2222.

INTERNATIONAL BICYCLE TOURS

The Fifty Plus Tour run by IBT is planned for people over 50 who are not into pedaling up mountains but love to cycle. The trip goes to Holland in May and takes you on a leisurely trip along bicycle paths and quiet country roads on flat terrain through farmland and quaint villages. You'll cover only about 30 miles a day, so there is plenty of time for sight-seeing, snacking, shopping, and relaxing. Although this is the only tour strictly limited to over-50s, many older bikers are found on IBT's other bike tours to Holland, Denmark, England, Ireland, Italy, France, Bermuda, Austria, Cape Cod, Charleston, the Chesapeake and Ohio Canal, and Florida. And, of course, many more sign on for Elderhostel's bike tours (in Bermuda, England, France, the Netherlands, Austria, and Denmark), all hosted by IBT.

For information: International Bicycle Tours, PO Box 754, Essex, CT 06426; 860-767-7005.

VERMONT BICYCLE TOURING

This venerable bike company has recently been acquired by Grand Circle Travel—a specialist in cultural, educational, and adventure vacations around the world for adventurers over the age of 50—which plans to tailor VBT's trips for this fast-growing age group. Although challenging routes will remain for those who want them, many of the itineraries will be less demanding and their schedules more relaxed. As a start, VBT's biking vacations currently include a number of trips eminently suitable for older bikers who seek adventure without all that much physical stress. One is the Salzburg Sojourn, which takes participants on flat bicycle paths and easy descents in the Austrian Alps. Another option is a tour of County Galway and the Connemara Coast in Ireland, visiting small villages, castles and pubs, lush forests, islands, and rocky ocean shores.

For information: VBT, PO Box 711, Bristol, VT 05443; 800-BIKE-TOUR (800-245-3868) or 803-453-4811.

WANDERING WHEELS

A program with a Christian perspective and "a strong biblical orientation," Wandering Wheels operates long-distance bike tours for all ages in this country and abroad, including a 40-day, 2,600-mile Breakaway Coast-to-Coast every spring that's geared specifically for people who are "middle age or older," as are the one-week fall specials that take you to a different locale every year.

For information: Wandering Wheels, PO Box 207, Upland, IN 46989; 765-998-7490.

WOMAN TOURS

A tour company specializing in bike trips for women only, Woman Tours reserves at least one trip a year for bikers over the age of 50. The current offering for this age group is a 56-day cross-country 3,135-mile adventure limited to 20 participants plus staff that starts pedaling in San Diego, California, and quits in St. Augustine, Florida. Mileage averages 50 to 70 miles a day, mostly on fairly flat terrain, with one rest day a week. Most nights are spent in motels or B&Bs, but a few are under the stars in state parks. A van carries the luggage, repair equipment, and you, if necessary.

Not ready for that? Woman Tours also schedules shorter bike trips, usually a week in length, for all ages. Currently, they occur in such locations as the Canadian Rockies, the canyons of the Southwest, Vermont, the Natchez Trace in Mississippi, California's Napa Valley, and the Kentucky bluegrass country.

For information: Woman Tours, PO Box 931, Driggs, ID 83422; 800-247-1444 or 208-354-8804.

TENNIS, ANYONE?

An estimated three million of the nation's tennis players are over 50, with the number increasing every year as more of us decide to forego rocking chairs for a few fast sets on the courts. You need only a court, a racquet, a can of balls, and an opponent to play tennis, but, if you'd like to be competitive or sociable, you may want to get into some senior tournaments.

UNITED STATES TENNIS ASSOCIATION

The USTA offers a wide variety of tournaments for players over the advanced age of 35, at both local and national levels. To participate, you must be a member ($25 per year). When you join, you will become a member of a regional section, receive periodic schedules of USTA-sponsored tournaments and events in your area for which you can sign up, get a discount on tennis books and publications, and receive a monthly magazine and a free subscription to *Tennis* magazine.

In the schedule of tournaments, you'll find competitions listed for specific five-year age groups: for men from 35 to 85-plus and for women from 35 to 80-plus. There are also self-rated tournaments that match you up with people of all ages who play at your level. If you feel you're good enough to compete, send for an application and sign up. There is usually a modest fee.

For information: USTA, 70 W. Red Oak Lane, White Plains, NY 10604-3602; 914-696-7000.

USTA LEAGUE TENNIS, SENIOR DIVISION

If you want to compete with other 50-plus tennis players

in local, area, and sectional competitions on four different surfaces culminating in a national championship, join the Senior Division of the USTA League Tennis program. Your level of play will be rated in a specific skill category ranging from beginner to advanced, and you'll compete only with people on your own ability level. Sign up in your community or write to the USTA for details.

For information: USTA, 70 W. Red Oak Lane, White Plains, NY 10604-3602; 914-696-7000.

USTA PLAY TENNIS AMERICA

The USTA Play Tennis America program is designed to encourage adult beginners, especially those over 50, to learn how to play the game. Available in many communities all over the country in public parks and tennis clubs, this is a three-stage instructional program, with each stage lasting three weeks (three hours a week). You'll learn basic tennis skills and practice playing in low-key competitions.

For information: USTA, 70 W. Red Oak Lane, White Plains, NY 10604-3602; 914-696-7000.

VAN DER MEER TENNIS UNIVERSITY

Van der Meer Tennis University offers five-day Seniors Clinics from September to May every year at its center on Hilton Head Island. Specifically for 50-plus players, beginning or experienced, the clinics provide more than 16 hours of instruction, including video analysis, tactics and strategies for singles and doubles, match play drills, plus round robins, social activities, and free court time. The goal is to improve your strokes and game strategy and show you how to get

more enjoyment out of your game. Discounted accommodations are available for participants. If you attend a clinic
on a nonsenior week or weekend, you will get a 10 percent
discount by showing your AARP card. And with an American Express Senior Member card, you'll get a $100 gift
cheque to spend while you're there.

For information: Van der Meer Tennis University, PO Box
5902, Hilton Head Island, SC 29938-5902; 800-845-6138
or 803-785-8388.

WALKING TOURS

There are so many organizations offering walking/hiking
trips designed for or eminently suited to mature travelers
that we can't list them all here. The following, however, spe-
cialize in travel on foot. Other walking trips are mentioned
throughout the book. Get yourself in shape for the
hikes by walking 10 miles or more every week for at least
a month.

APPALACHIAN MOUNTAIN CLUB

Every year this famous hiking club, the oldest conservation and recreation organization in the U.S., schedules a
few inexpensive 2- to 5-day treks especially for people over
the age of 50. You'll hike two to eight miles at an easy
pace in these lush mountains and valleys and sleep in
rustic mountain huts at night, with plenty of time to savor
the scenery and glimpse the wildlife. Routes vary from
year to year and sometimes include trips for women only.
Check out the Silver Sneakers Walking Weekend in

New Hampshire in fall foliage season, spring hiking in the White Mountains, and a special traverse of the "high huts."
For information: Appalachian Mountain Club, 20 Joy St., Boston, MA 02108; 617-523-0636.

ELDERHOSTEL WALKING PROGRAMS

Elderhostel's special international programs include two-week walking tours for which participants must be highly ambulatory and in good overall health. Accompanied by guides, lecturers, and local specialists, the walkers, carrying small day packs, take daily walks ranging from 4 to 12 miles a day, rain or shine, on predominantly level trails but with occasional steep sections and steps. You'll stay and dine in small hotels, while lunch is taken en route. Current destinations are Bermuda, the Austrian and Italian Tyrol, northern England, and Switzerland. Trekking trips are also on Elderhostel's menu, taking you up to eight miles a day on footpaths over Nepal's mountainous terrain. For these you must be in even better physical shape and accustomed to vigorous exercise.
For information: Elderhostel, 75 Federal St., Boston, MA 02110; 617-426-7788.

ELDERTREKS

On these trekking trips in exotic lands, most of them in the Far East, you will hike overland on foot and, in many cases, sleep on an air mattress in a tribal village house or a tent. The trips are rated for difficulty so you may choose one that matches your abilities. For more, see Chapter 5.

For information: ElderTreks, 597 Markham St., Toronto, ON M6G 2L7; 800-741-7956 or 416-588-5000.

50+ MOUNTAIN TOURS

Ten-day guided camping and hiking tours of the Canadian Rocky Mountains for active adventurers over 50 are the specialty of this company. Your group of no more than eight participants served by four staff members spends three days at each of three campsites in the Banff, Columbia Icefields, and Lake Louise areas, settling down in large stand-up tents furnished with comfortable cots and eating meals at tables in a dining tent. Each day, you have your choice of graded hikes, ranging from easy strolls to strenuous all-day hikes deep into the mountains. A van takes you from site to site and on sight-seeing drives.

For information: 50+ Mountain Tours Ltd., Box 2, Site 3, RR1, Priddis, AB T0L 1W0; 403-931-2208.

INTERHOSTEL

Interhostel's collection of educational trips for people over 50 now includes a few walking programs in Bordeaux and the Dordogne Valley of France, another in the Tuscany region of Italy, and others in Scotland and Ireland. Moving from place to place by van or bus, you'll set forth on foot to explore, taking leisurely walking tours wherever you go. You'll cover perhaps three to five miles a day, sometimes on unpaved, uneven rocky terrain with stairs and moderate hills, so be sure you are an enthusiastic walker. See Chapter 16 for more about Interhostel programs.

For information: Interhostel, University of New Hampshire, 6 Garrison Ave., Durham, NH 03824; 800-733-9753 or 603-862-1147.

OVERSEAS ADVENTURE TRAVEL

OAT, which runs adventure trips all over the globe, has introduced European walking tours designed especially for the active mature traveler. Everything's included, even airfare, on these leisurely 12-day guided strolls through the hill towns of Tuscany, the Cotswolds, Provence, Scotland, or Switzerland. You'll stay in small inns and take morning and afternoon walks, drive to historic places, and experience the local culture up close. A support van goes along to carry drinks, snacks, lunch, and weary walkers.

For information: Overseas Adventure Travel, 625 Mt. Auburn St., Cambridge, MA 02138; 800-221-0814 or 617-876-0533.

RIVER ODYSSEYS WEST

If you love wilderness rivers but aren't into whitewater rafting (see Chapter 3), consider ROW's raft-supported walking tours along trails that follow the course of the Middle Fork of the Salmon River in Idaho or the Snake River in Hells Canyon. Carrying only a day pack and led by a guide, you hike six or eight miles a day with plenty of time to smell the flowers and spot the wildlife. A cargo raft carries all the camping gear and your luggage as well as the food and other supplies, and a smaller support raft floats along at the group's pace to act as a sag wagon for tired walkers. When you arrive at camp each afternoon, the staff has already set up the roomy tents and the kitchen and has started cook-

ing dinner, giving you time to relax, fish, or explore.
For information: River Odysseys West, PO Box 579-UD,
Coeur d'Alene, ID 83816-0579; 800-451-6034 or 208-765-
0841.

SHOTT'S WALKS IN THE WEST

On these guided walking trips exclusively for people over
the age of 50, you'll explore places you'd never see from a
car or a bus, have close encounters with the scenic West,
get your exercise, and have time left over for sight-seeing
and shopping. But you won't be spending the nights in a
sleeping bag under the stars—you'll sleep in a comfortable
bed in a lodge or a motel, complete with bathroom. Recent
walks have taken place in Arches and Canyonlands National
Parks, Olympic National Park, the San Diego coastal area,
the Colorado Rockies, Taos, and the Grand Tetons.

Trips are limited to six guests per guide and you carry
only your own day pack. If you can walk comfortably for
about 10 miles a week, you're in shape for these hikes.
For information: Shott's Walks in the West, PO Box 51106,
Colorado Springs, CO 80949; 719-531-9577.

SIERRA CLUB

Don't sign up for the club's backpacking trip in the Carson-
Iceberg Wilderness in California if you've been living a
sedentary life, advises the Sierra Club. That's because even
though it is for grandparents and their grandchildren, it is
definitely strenuous. If you still want to know about it, see
Chapter 3.
For information: Sierra Club Outing Dept., 85 Second St.,
San Francisco, CA 94105; 415-977-5522.

WALK YOUR WAY

The walking tours led by Rosemary Davenport in her native England always include a few trips a year designated for seniors. These are 12-day tours of quaint and picturesque places on the Isle of Wight, the Lake District, the Dales of Yorkshire, Dorset, or the Cotswolds. Walks are circular, covering up to 10 miles a day on flat and rolling terrain. You'll visit a different village each day.

Some of this agency's tours for all ages are also suitable for mature walkers who are in good enough shape to cope with more miles and a few ascents.

For information: Walk Your Way, PO Box 231, Red Feather Lakes, CO 80545; 970-881-2709.

WALKING THE WORLD

Anyone who loves adventure, is at least 50 years old, and is in good physical shape is invited to participate in Walking the World's explorations. These are 7- to 17-day backcountry treks, covering 6 to 10 miles a day, that focus on natural and cultural history. On some trips, you'll camp out and, carrying only a day pack, hike to each new destination. On others, you will lodge in cabins, small country inns, or B&Bs, setting forth on daily walks into the countryside. Groups are small, from 12 to 18 participants plus two local guides, and there's no upper age limit. No previous hiking experience is necessary, but obviously you need to be in good physical shape.

Destinations include Arches and Canyonlands National Parks in Utah; Banff and Jasper National Parks in the Canadian Rockies; plus trips in Scotland, England, Wales, Switzerland, Ireland, New Zealand, Maine, Hawaii, Tahiti, Costa Rica, and Italy.

For information: Walking the World, PO Box 1186, Fort Collins, CO 80522; 800-340-9255 or 498-225-0500.

EXPLORING BY SNOWMOBILE
SENIOR WORLD TOURS

Travel with your contemporaries on snowmobiles through Wyoming's Tetons and Yellowstone Park on these seniors-only adventures. Home base is Cowboy Village Resort at Togwotee, 50 miles out of Jackson, where you'll stay in a cabin or lodge. Snowmobiles; snowmobile suits with boots, gloves, and helmets; cross-country skis; and all meals are included. As part of the package, you'll get driving lessons before setting out with a guide to explore the wilderness. Traveling from inn to inn, you will cover many miles and enjoy spectacular scenery for 6 or 8 days.

No special expertise is required, but don't even think of it unless you're in good physical condition.

For information: Senior World Tours, 2205 N. River Rd., Fremont, OH 43420; 888-355-1686.

SNOWSHOEING
APPALACHIAN MOUNTAIN CLUB

In addition to its hiking trips, AMC, a leader in backcountry and environmental education, mountain ecology, and river research, offers a couple of three-day weekend snowshoe adventures for over-50s—one for beginners, the other for intermediates. You can try new skills and practice old ones while you explore the forests. You must be in good shape and capable of carrying a full day pack, including food.

For information: Appalachian Mountain Club, 20 Joy St., Boston, MA 02108; 617-523-0636.

MOTORCYCLE HEAVEN
BEACH'S MOTORCYCLE ADVENTURES

If motorcycling is your passion and adventure is in your blood, look into motorcycle tours offered by the Beaches, a family that's been conducting cycling tours since 1972. All ages, including yours, may choose among several itineraries including the Alpine Adventure through the mountains of Germany, Austria, Italy, Switzerland, and France; the Maori Meander in the backcountry of New Zealand; and the Viking Vector along the Norwegian coast. Motorcycles, all BMWs, are provided in your choice of available models and there is no mileage charge. Your luggage is carried by a van. By the way, both bikes and automobiles are welcome on these tours, so if friends or family want to join you they may go along in a car.

You're on your own during the day, following a tour book that gives daily itineraries, road maps, distances, estimated en route times, business hours, sight-seeing ideas, good (and bad) roads, suggestions for activities, driving tips, and directions to the hotel of the night. The daily routing, pace, and stops are up to you. There are several riding options for each day, so you may decide to cruise along or ride long and hard. Every evening, however, you'll meet the group and your guide at a comfortable hotel or family farm where you'll eat dinner that night and have breakfast the next morning.

For information: Beach's Motorcycle Adventures, 2763 W. River Parkway, Grand Island, NY 14072; 716-773-4960.

RETREADS MOTORCYCLE CLUB

Retreads, an association of motorcycle enthusiasts who have reached the ripe old age of at least 40, get together for state, regional, and international rallies to talk cycling and ride together. Each state association also schedules weekly or monthly gatherings. Started as a correspondence club in 1969, it has grown to over 20,000 members—men and women—in the U.S., Canada, and several other countries including Japan, England, and Australia. Annual contribution is $10 a year per person or $15 per couple. A club newsletter keeps members informed of the activities.

For information: Retreads Motorcycle Club International, 528 North Main St., Albany, IN 47320; 765-789-4070 or 941-351-7199 (November 1 to May 30).

CANOE VACATIONS
GUNFLINT NORTHLAND OUTFITTERS

These outfitters, with paddling adventures on the remote lakes of the Boundary Waters Wilderness Area between Minnesota and Ontario, the largest waterways wilderness in the world, schedule several one-week trips every summer expressly for seniors. With a guide, you paddle and portage your canoe deep into heavily forested areas, home to moose, beaver, mink, loons, and other creatures of the wild. One option is a seven-night package limited to eight guests that includes two nights at Gunflint Lodge and five nights camping with complete outfitting. Camp is set up for you, and your meals—perhaps including the fish you've caught—are cooked over the campfire by your guide. The second choice is a lodge-to-lodge trip that combines three nights at the Lodge, one night at a rustic inn on an island across the border in Canada, and the others exploring and camping in the wilderness. Yet another option is gathering a few friends and setting up your own special trip.

For information: Gunflint Northland Outfitters, 750 Gunflint Trail, Grand Marais, MN 55604; 800-362-5251.

KAYAKING TOURS

NEW ZEALAND ADVENTURES

Here's your chance to take a five-day sea kayak tour among the six main islands in the Bay of Islands in New Zealand. This is a relaxed tour specifically for you and your peers over 50, and the only criteria for participation is that you are in good health and enjoy an active vacation. You'll stay in a cabin in Otehei Bay on Urupukapuka Island, eat home-cooked meals, and travel with a knowledgeable local kayak guide. You'll paddle three to five miles a day by kayak exploring the volcanic rock formations and sea caves, take day hikes on island trails, swim, snorkel, sail, and become acquainted with the Maori culture. Trips are scheduled in our winter, New Zealand's summer. For more vigorous tent camping adventures, join a tour "for all ages."

For information: New Zealand Adventures, HCR 56 Box 575, John Day, OR 97845; 541-932-4925.

GOLFING VACATIONS

GREENS FEES

Most municipal and many private golf courses offer senior golfers (usually those over 65) a discount off the regular greens fees. Take your identification with you and always make inquiries before you play.

GOLF ACADEMY OF HILTON HEAD ISLAND

If you have an American Express Senior Member Card (see Chapter 10), you may sign up for any of the Golf Academy's multiple-day golf schools at Sea Pines Plantation in Hilton Head with a 15 percent discount on the cost. You'll get instruction on everything from full swings and chipping to flop shots, and play 18 holes at the Harbour Town Golf Links.

For information: Golf Academy of Hilton Head Island, PO Box 5580, Hilton Head Island, SC 29938; 800-925-0467.

THE GOLF CARD

Designed especially for senior golfers, the Golf Card entitles members to two complimentary rounds of golf a year at over 3,300 affilliated courses in the country, up to half off the player's fees at 300 additional courses, and savings at golf resorts in the U.S., Canada, the Bahamas, Jamaica, and the Dominican Republic. Membership fees are $95 the first year for a single or $145 for two, thereafter $85 a year for a single and $135 for a double.

Other benefits to cardholders: a Quest International Card good for 50 percent off on hotels and 25 percent off on meals, and a subscription to *Golf Traveler*, a magazine that serves as a guide to the participating courses and resorts.

For information: The Golf Card, PO Box 7022, Englewood, CO 80155; 800-321-8269 or 303-790-2267.

NATIONAL SENIOR SPORTS ASSOCIATION (NSSA)

More than 3,000 golfers over 50—average age 63—belong to NSSA, which sponsors recreational and competitive four-day midweek golf holidays once a month at highly rated courses all over the country. The holidays include accommodations, golf (including a 54-hole medal-play tournament), breakfasts, at least two dinners, and activities for nonplaying companions. Recent locations have included Pebble Beach Resorts in California; Kings Mill Resort in Williamsburg; Greenbriar in White Sulphur Springs, West Virginia; and Palmilla Resort in Los Cobos, Mexico. Longer golf holidays are scheduled once a year to more far-flung locations such as Ireland and Scotland, Portugal, Canada, and Hawaii.

Membership in NSSA costs $25 a year, includes your spouse, entitles you to participate in the trips, and gets you a voluminous monthly newsletter. It also includes a $100 certificate to use toward your first trip of the year and discounts on travel and selected golf courses around the country.

For information: NSSA, 83 Princeton Ave., Hopewell, NJ 08525; 800-282-6772 or 609-466-0022.

JOHN JACOBS GOLF SCHOOLS

Golfers over the age of 62 get a discount of 10 percent on the cost of golf vacations offered July through December at any John Jacobs Golf School. You'll learn how to improve your game while you play at some of the finest courses in the country. Most packages include lodging, breakfast and dinner, instruction, course time, greens fees, and cart.
For information: John Jacobs Golf Schools, 800-472-5007.

EVENTS FOR RAPID RUNNERS
FIFTY-PLUS FITNESS ASSOCIATION

This is not a club, although it occasionally sponsors athletic events for its over-50 members. It is an organization formed by eminent exercise researchers at Stanford University for the exchange of information about physical exercise and its benefits (and hazards) among the older population. Its members, from almost every state and several foreign countries, also serve as volunteers for ongoing studies of such activities as running, swimming, biking, and racewalking. Each is asked to contribute $35 a year, tax-deductible, to defray costs. The association sponsors many events in the California Bay Area. These include walks, runs, swims, bike rides, and seminars and conferences on aging.
For information: Fifty-Plus Fitness Association, PO Box D, Stanford, CA 94309; 650-323-6160.

OVER-50 SOFTBALL

INTERNATIONAL SENIOR SOFTBALL ASSOCIATION

ISSA, an association that was founded to promote softball for men and women over the age of 50, conducts the World Championship Tournaments for over 300 senior teams every year in northern Virginia. Players who are members of senior leagues and local softball associations all over the U.S. may join, and so may individuals without affiliation. Members receive a master nationwide tournament schedule, the results of all national tournaments, and the rankings of all senior softball teams.

For information: ISSA, 9401 East St., Manassas, VA 20110; 703-368-1188.

NATIONAL ASSOCIATION OF SENIOR CITIZEN SOFTBALL

The NASCS is an association of several thousand softball players and hundreds of teams in the U.S. and Canada, with a goal of promoting a worldwide interest in senior softball. To play ball on one of its teams, you must be at least 50 years old. There's no upper age limit, and both men and women are welcomed. NASCS runs about 15 tournaments every year in the U.S. plus one in Canada and is the organizer of the annual Senior Softball World Series, a tournament for players who must first qualify in local competitions. Every year more than 100 teams from the U.S. and Canada compete in a major ballpark. A quarterly magazine keeps members up to date on happenings here and abroad.

For information: NASCS, PO Box 1085, Mt. Clemens, MI 48046; 810-792-2110.

SENIOR SOFTBALL USA

This organization, the largest senior softball group in the world, conducts softball tournaments all over the country and organizes international tournaments as well, including the Senior Softball World Championship Games held in September. Anyone over 50, man or woman, in the U.S. and Canada may join and many thousands have. Members get assistance finding teams in their areas and may subscribe to the *Senior Softball USA News*, which keeps them up to date on tournaments and other news. They are eligible to take part in an annual international tour that takes teams to play ball in foreign lands.

For information: Senior Softball USA, 7052 Riverside Blvd., Sacramento, CA 95831; 916-393-8566.

SENIOR GAMES

NATIONAL SENIOR GAMES ASSOCIATION

Sponsored by major corporations, NSGA promotes health and fitness for seniors through competitive multisport events held across the country, including the National Senior Games, a competition that takes place in a different location every two years. In 1997, it was held at the University of Arizona in Tucson. In 1999, it will be at Walt Disney World in Orlando.

To qualify for the events—from track and field, swimming, cycling, golf, tennis, and bowling to volleyball, horseshoes, archery, running, badminton, softball, racquetball, triathlon, and table tennis—athletes must first qualify in authorized state competitions across the country. The events are organized for men and women in five-year age brackets from 50 to 100-plus.

If you want to be ready to go for the next senior games, get the ground rules from your local senior sports organization or the national headquarters.

For a free list of local and state games all over the country, write to NSGA at the address below. You'll find a representative sample of these games in the following pages. *For information:* NSGA, 445 North Blvd., Ste. 2001, Baton Rouge, LA 70802; 504-379-7337.

HUNTSMAN WORLD SENIOR GAMES

Every October, a few thousand athletes—male and female, 50 and over, from the U.S. and many other countries—gather in St. George, Utah, for two weeks of competition in 19 events from basketball, mountain biking, golf, swimming, and tennis to track and field and triathlon. In addition to athletic events, the games try to foster health, friendship, and world peace through healthy-lifestyle seminars and free health screenings. Included are social events such as receptions, band concerts, and ceremonial dinners. *For information:* Huntsman World Senior Games, 82 W. 700 South, St. George, UT 84770; 800-562-1268 or 801-674-0550.

STATE AND LOCAL SENIOR GAMES

Most states hold their own senior games once or twice a year and send their best competitors to national events. If you don't find your state among those listed here, that doesn't mean there's no program in your area—many are sponsored by counties, cities, even local agencies and colleges. Check with your local city, county, or state recreation departments to see what's going on near you or contact the NSGA for a free list. You don't have to be a serious competitor to enter these games but merely ready to enjoy yourself. So what if you don't go home with a medal? At the very least, you'll meet other energetic people and have a lot of laughs.

ARIZONA

If you are over 50, male or female, you are eligible to participate in the Flagstaff Senior Olympics held over four days every year in September. You may compete in events that include bowling, cycling, golf, handball, racewalking, swimming, tennis, track and field, powerlifting, and more. Sign up for the festivities, which include an evening social and tickets to a Northern Arizona University football game. Medals are awarded for each event.

For information: Flagstaff Senior Olympics, PO Box 5063, Flagstaff, AZ 86011; 520-523-3560.

CALIFORNIA

Hundreds of senior athletes from all over the United States and Canada compete for 10 days in February in the annual Palm Springs Senior Olympics International. The sporting events range from track and field to golf and tennis, with medal winners going on to compete in the National Senior Olympics. If you are 50 or more, a resident or a visitor to the state, you are eligible to participate.

For information: Senior Olympics International, Palm

Springs, Mizell Senior Center, 480 S. Sunrise Way, Palm Springs, CA 92262; 760-323-5689.

On the last weekend in February each year, the Running Springs Senior Winter Games are held at a resort in the San Bernardino National Forest. Open to anyone over the age of 50, the competitions include skiing, ice skating, ice fishing, snowball throwing, snowshoe racing, and a few indoor games such as billiards, bridge, and table tennis. Social events are included. There is a modest registration fee plus a small additional fee for each event entered.

For information: Running Springs Senior Winter Games, PO Box 3333, Running Springs, CA 92382; 909-867-3176.

COLORADO

The Senior Winter Games at the Summit take place each year during three days in the second week of February in the quaint Victorian village of Breckenridge. Anyone from anywhere who's over 55 and wants to compete against peers is welcome. Events include cross-country skiing, downhill slalom, speed skating, snowshoe races, biathlon, figure skating, and more, plus social activities. Age categories for the competitions begin at 55 to 59 and increase in five-year increments to 90-plus. A registration fee that allows you to participate in as many events as you wish currently stands at $25.

The summertime Rocky Mountain Senior Games take place in Greeley, Colorado, every August and include many events ranging from running to swimming, dancing, and tennis.

For information: Senior Winter Games at the Summit, PO

Box 442, Breckenridge, CO 80424; 970-453-2461. Or for the Rocky Mountain Senior Games: Rocky Mountain Senior Games, 1010 6th St., Greeley, CO 80631; 970-350-9433.

CONNECTICUT

The Connecticut Senior Olympics include not only competitive sport events but also a mini health fair and many physical fitness activities. Residents of Connecticut and neighboring states who are 55-plus converge on the University of Bridgeport on the first weekend in June for three days of events such as the 5,000-meter run, the 100-yard dash, the mile run, the long jump, diving, bocci, and tennis. These summer games require a small entrance fee.

The one-day Connecticut Senior Winter Olympics, usually held in March, are open to anyone from anywhere who's 55 and an amateur. The games feature downhill, giant slalom, cross-country, and snowshoe races, and take place at Ski Sundown.

For information: Connecticut Senior Olympics, PO Box 790, Milldale, CT 06467; 860-621-4661.

FLORIDA

The Golden Age Games in Sanford are the biggest and the oldest senior games in the country. Held annually in November, they go on for a week and include plenty of competitions, ceremonies, social events, and entertainments. If you are over 50, you are eligible to participate regardless of residency. In other words, you needn't be a Florida resident to compete for the gold, silver, and bronze medals in such sports as basketball, biking, bowling, canoeing, checkers, diving, dance, swimming, tennis, triathlon, track and field, canasta, and croquet. There is a small entry fee for each event.

For information: Golden Age Games, PO Box 1298, Sanford, FL 32772; 407-330-5697.

MICHIGAN

Michigan Senior Olympics, a four-day happening open to people 50 and older, are held every year on the campus of a state college. For small registration and event fees, you get a chance to compete for medals in athletic events from archery to volleyball. You may also take home ribbons for your baking skills, arts and crafts, and dancing. Spectators are welcomed too.

For information: Michigan Senior Olympics, 312 Woodward, Rochester, MI 48307; 810-608-0250.

MISSOURI

The St. Louis Senior Olympics have become an institution in Missouri by now. A four-day event that is open to anyone who lives anywhere and is 50 years old, it costs a nominal amount and is action-oriented. No knitting contests here—only energetic events such as bicycle races, 200-meter races, standing long jumps, golf, basketball, tennis singles and doubles, and swimming.

For information: Senior Olympics, JCCA, 2 Millstone Campus, St. Louis, MO 63146; 314-432-6780, Ext. 188.

MONTANA

Men and women over the age of 50, from Montana or otherwise, are invited to participate in the Montana Senior Olympics held every year in June. Events range from archery, badminton, bowling, and basketball to swimming, tennis, softball, and track.

For information: Montana Senior Olympics, 3621 Ft. Laramie Ave., Billings, MT 59102; 406-252-2795.

NEW HAMPSHIRE

For three days in September, you can compete with your peers in the Granite State Senior Summer Games, which feature 15 sports events ranging from swimming to tennis, track and field, shuffleboard, and table tennis. In alternate years, these are qualifying games for the U.S. Senior Sports Classic. Sign up if you are at least 50 and in good operating condition. The cost is minimal. Regional games are also scheduled throughout the state during the summer.

The Granite State Senior Winter Games, held in Waterville Valley for three days in March, are open to men and women 50 and over who compete in groups of five-year increments. They get a chance to challenge their peers in dual slalom, giant slalom, and cross-country races. Other events include speed skating, snowball throw, hockey goal shoot, and snowshoe races. Everyone in the appropriate age range is welcome to enter the competitions and attend both an opening reception and an awards banquet. Costs for entry, lift tickets, fees, rentals, and social affairs are low. Inexpensive lodging is also available.

For information: Granite State Senior Winter Games, PO Box 1942, Rochester, NH 03866; 603-332-0055.

NEW YORK

The Empire State Senior Games, open to all New York residents who are 50 or over, are held in Syracuse over three days in June. Winners may qualify for the National Senior Olympics. For a small registration fee, amateur athletes may compete in many events that range from swimming to bridge, basketball, softball, croquet, track and field, tennis, racewalking, cycling, and more. There are additional fees for golf and bowling. Participants are invited to social events each of the three nights.

For information: Empire State Senior Games, NYS Parks, 6105 E. Seneca Turnpike, Jamesville, NY 13078; 315-492-9654.

NORTH CAROLINA

After local games are held statewide, the winners travel to Raleigh for the North Carolina Senior Games State Finals and, perhaps, on to the national games. Most sports are on the agenda, plus an arts competition that celebrates artists in heritage, literary, performing, and visual arts. The state also sponsors the SilverStriders, a walking club for those 50 or better that gives its members logbooks for tracking progress, gifts and awards, and an annual report of their accomplishments.

For information: North Carolina Senior Games, PO Box 33590, Raleigh, NC 27636; 919-851-5456.

PENNSYLVANIA

The Keystone Senior Games "combine sports, recreation, and entertainment with fellowship." You can get some of each if you are a Pennsylvania resident who is 50 or older. The games are held over five days in July at a university campus where you can get lodging and three meals a day at low cost. If you prefer to stay in a motel, you'll get a senior discount.

For information: Keystone Senior Games, 31 S. Hancock St., Wilkes Barre, PA 18702; 717-823-3164.

VERMONT

If you are over 50 and an amateur in your sport, you are invited to participate in the Green Mountain Senior Games. At the summer games held in September at Green Mountain College in Poultney, the competitive events—organized in age groups from 50 to 95-plus—include everything from golf and tennis to swimming, darts, horseshoes, walking, running, table tennis, bowling, croquet, softball, basketball, and mountain biking. And just for fun, there are scenic walks, socials, and free swims.

For information: Green Mountain Senior Games, 131 Holden Hill Rd., Weston, VT 05161; 802-824-6521.

VIRGINIA

The Virginia Senior Games are an annual four-day event held each spring on a college campus, where older athletes compete to qualify for the U.S. National Senior Olympics— or just for the fun of it. It is a combination of social events and entertainment with sports competitions, open to Virginia residents over the age of 50. Spouses are invited to come along and enjoy the hospitality, which includes parties, dances, tours of local sites, and other festivities. The fees are low, lodging and meals are cheap, and the sporting events are many, ranging from rope jumping, miniature golf, and riflery to swimming, running, and tennis for age groups from 55 upwards.

For information: Virginia Senior Games, Virginia Recreation and Park Society, 6038 Cold Harbor Rd., Mechanicsville, VA; 804-730-9447.

14

Adventures on Skis

VER THE TOP

Downhill skiing is one sport you'd think would appeal only to less mature, less wise, less breakable people. On the contrary, there is an astounding number of ardent over-50 skiers who would much rather glide down mountains than sit around waiting for springtime. In fact, many of us ski more than ever now that we're older because we can go midweek when the crowds are thinner and we get impressive discounts on lift tickets. And a lot of us are taking up the sport for the first time. Ski schools all over the United States and Canada are reporting an increase of older students in beginner classes.

The truth is, you're never too old to learn how to ski or to improve your technique. Once you get the hang of it, you can ski at your own speed, choosing the terrain, the difficulty level, and the challenge. You can swoop down cliffs through narrow icy passes or wend your way on gentle slopes in a more leisurely fashion, aided by the new improved skis and boots, clearly marked and carefully groomed trails, and sophisticated lifts that take all the work out of getting up the mountain.

Besides, ski resorts are falling all over themselves catering to older skiers, offering discounts, cheap season passes, and other engaging incentives. In fact, it is a rare ski area that does not give a break to skiers over a certain age.

PROGRAMS FOR MATURE SKIERS

THE OVER THE HILL GANG

OTHG began as a ski club (three former Colorado ski instructors were looking for company on the slopes), and skiing is still its major activity. If you are 50, you are eligible to join (your spouse may be younger) and enjoy the club's ski adventures on this continent and abroad. You pay special group rates and sometimes receive free guides and special lift-line privileges. In addition, at many ski areas, even when you ski on your own you will get "senior" discounts like those offered skiers over 65 on lift tickets, rentals, lessons, and packages. People who have never put on a pair of skis or haven't tried them in years can take advantage of Learn to Ski programs, refresher clinics, or group lessons.

Every year OTHG schedules at least 20 escorted Senior Ski Week packages in the West plus more to foreign destinations. And when the ski season ends, you may join the Gang for a bike trip, a party, whitewater rafting, hiking, or golfing. This club, with an average age of 64, is definitely out for a good time.

Local OTHG chapters also run their own ski trips and all members everywhere are invited to go along. At some ski areas, local and visiting members meet once a week to ski together. At Breckenridge in Colorado, for example, they gather on Tuesdays to ski all day with their own guides and get together for lunch. At Keystone, it's every Thursday morning, and at Vail, Monday is the day for camaraderie.

National membership requires an annual fee of $40 ($65 per couple) plus chapter dues if you join a local Gang. **For information:** Over the Hill Gang International, 3310 Cedar Heights Dr., Dept. G, Colorado Springs, CO 80904; 719-685-4656.

SENIOR SKIER NETWORK

A group of 30 resorts throughout the East has joined together to offer midweek senior skier programs modeled after the Senior Skier Development Program at Ski Windham in New York. Each host mountain welcomes everybody over 50 to its full-day program, which includes clinics and ski instruction with four hours of on-snow lessons and other activities that vary from mountain to mountain. Cost is more than a lift ticket but less than a lift/lesson combination. Many of these areas also offer a Senior Program Package for the season. Each area's program feeds into the winter state games in Vermont, Connecticut, and Massachusetts.

For information: Professional Ski Instructors of America, Eastern Education Foundation, 1-A Lincoln Ave., Albany, NY 12205; 518-452-1166.

70+ SKI CLUB

You must be at least 70 years old and prove it before you may join this club with almost 14,000 members worldwide, all of them in their 70s, 80s, and 90s. Founded in 1977 by Lloyd Lambert, a 75-year-old avid skier and columnist, the club promotes the interests of senior skiers, especially those on limited incomes. Today, as a result, most ski areas give seniors free or half-price lift tickets.

The club plans several trips and events a year at ski resorts in the Northeast and the West, at least one in Europe, and others in New Zealand, Chile, or Argentina in our summer months. Hunter Mountain in New York hosts the club's annual meeting every March. Here the 70+ Ski Races have become such a popular event that contestants are divided into three age groups—men 70 to 80, women 70 to 80, and everyone over 80. Awards are presented at a gala party at the lodge.

Lifetime membership costs $5 ($15 for those outside the U.S. or Canada). Proof of your age is required with your application, and you may not apply earlier than two weeks before your 70th birthday. You will receive a patch, a membership card, a periodic newsletter, and a list of ski areas and their respective discounts for seniors.

For information: 70+ Ski Club, 1633 Albany St., Schenectady, NY 12304; 518-346-5505.

THE WILD OLD BUNCH

This merry band of senior skiers who navigate the steep slopes of Alta in Utah is an informal group of men and women from Utah and many other states who ski together for fun, welcoming anybody who wants to join them. There are no rules, no designated leaders, no lessons, no regular meetings, and no age restrictions, though most members are well past 50, retired business or professional people. Somewhere between 50 and 100 avid skiers now wear the Wild Old Bunch patch.

The group grows haphazardly as members pick up stray mature skiers they find on the slopes, showing them their mountain and passing along their enthusiasm for the steeper trails and the off-trail skiing in Alta's famous powder. Says a spokesperson, "If you visit Alta and would like to join in some of the old-fashioned camaraderie of skiing, just look for any of us on the slopes or on the deck of the mid-mountain Alpenglow Inn, where we gather for lunch and tales. Either ski with us or grab a seat for some lively conversation."

Although the bunch isn't sexist, some of the wives prefer to stay on less difficult slopes or to travel the cross-country trails, so they wear "Wild Wives" patches.

For information: Look for the Wild Old Bunch on the slopes.

ELDERHOSTEL SKI PROGRAMS

Both downhill and cross-country skiers can find Elderhostel programs in the U.S. and Canada that will teach you how to ski or help you improve your techniques. Sometimes the programs are exclusively ski-oriented, but more often skiing is just one of the courses offered. Check out the Elderhostel winter catalogs and take your choice. Currently, cross-country ski programs are offered at Banff National

Park in the Canadian Rockies, Finland, Norway, the Kaibab Forest in Utah, and Mesa Verde National Park in Colorado. Downhill programs are given, among other places, at Sunday River in Maine, Silver Creek Ski Resort in the Colorado Rockies, Sundance Ski Resort in Utah, and Smuggler's Notch in Vermont.

For information: Elderhostel, 75 Federal St., Boston, MA 02110; 617-426-7788. In Canada: Elderhostel Canada, 5 Cataraqui St., Kingston, ON K7K 1Z7; 613-530-2222.

MORE GOOD DEALS FOR DOWNHILL SKIERS

The older you are, the less it costs to ski. There's hardly a ski area in North America today that doesn't give mature skiers a good deal. Many cut the price of lift tickets in half for skiers at age 65, and most stop charging altogether at 70, although a couple—Alta in Utah and Mt. Tom in Massachusetts—make you wait until you're 80 to ski free. A few areas charge anybody over the age of 65 only $5 a day to ski, and most make offers on season passes that are hard to refuse. Others plan special senior programs specifically for mature skiers.

To give you an idea of what's out there, here is a sampling of the special senior programs, workshops, and clubs in the states where skiing is big business. This list does not include all areas, of course, so be sure to check out others in locations that interest you. Remember to carry proof of age with you at all times. The ski areas change their programs every year or so, too; so, using the following information as a guide, you must do some of your own research.

CALIFORNIA

Ski in California and you'll get good deals on lift tickets and season passes almost everywhere. Plus, there are some special programs designed especially for mature skiers, such as the following.

Tahoe Donner Downhill Ski Area schedules ski clinics for skiers over the age of 50 every Tuesday morning. The inexpensive package for beginners and experienced skiers includes a lift ticket, continental breakfast, three hours of ski lessons, and a videotape review of your skiing technique.

At Northstar-at-Tahoe, the three-day Golden Stars Clinic has been tailored for skiers over 60 of intermediate or better ability who want to improve their skills on the slopes. Offered several times a winter, the clinic provides three-hour morning lessons, all-day lift tickets, and video analysis.

At Heavenly Ski Resort, there are free four-hour workshops for skiers over 55. And Mammoth Mountain offers three-day senior ski clinics.

And at Squaw Valley, anybody over 60 may ski all day for only $5.

The senior program at Bear Valley, in the Sierra Nevada Mountains between Lake Tahoe and Yosemite, is even better. At 65, you may ski free any day, any time. If you prefer a season pass, you can get one for just $10.

COLORADO

Every ski area in Colorado offers discounted lift tickets to seniors, some starting at 60, others at 65. Most charge nothing at all to ski after 70. And there are many special programs, lessons, and clubs especially designed for mature skiers. For example:

At Breckenridge, two-day Silver Skiing Seminars for skiers over 50 of all abilities, taught by seniors, include lift tickets, lessons, video analysis, and a group dinner. Breckenridge is the place where members of the local Over The Hill Gang, plus any other visitors 50 and over, get together on Tuesdays for a day on the slopes with their own guide. Breckenridge also hosts the Senior Winter Games at the Summit for three days in February.

It's Thursday mornings at Keystone for Gang members and visitors to ski with volunteer guides.

At Vail, any skier over 50 is welcome to meet on Mondays and ski with OTHG members. At Steamboat, together with volunteer guides, they gang up on the slopes every day from Sunday through Thursday. At Copper Mountain, they usually meet four days a week and take part in ski clinics and social events. At all of the mountains, all 50-plus skiers, members or not, are invited along.

Silver Creek Resort offers Never-Ever 50+, a learn-to-ski program exclusively for mature people who have never been on skis before. Scheduled on Wednesday and Saturday mornings, it includes lesson, equipment, and lift ticket.

Sunlight Mountain Resort in Glenwood Springs has its 100 Club, open to couples whose combined ages total 100 years or more, or singles who are 50 or older. Club members meet each Wednesday to ski in the morning and stay for lunch.

Crested Butte Mountain, too, has one-day senior workshops for beginners to advanced skiers, and a senior women's group called the Crested Butte Beauties welcomes visitors and locals. At Eldora, skiers and snowboarders 65 and older can participate in Senior Ski every Tuesday. Senior Days at Ski Cooper gives you a day lift ticket, free racing and an après-ski party. Telluride's Master Club race program for seniors meets on Saturdays for lessons on gate training, carving techniques, and speed.

The SnoMasters Classic at Purgatory, for skiers 55 and over, is a four-day event held twice every winter, providing discounted lessons by instructors of your own generation, breakfast each morning, and a party.

IDAHO

The famous Sun Valley Resort reserves two weeks every January as Prime Time Specials, when skiers over 60 get a break on lift tickets and accommodations. Included in the package are seven nights' lodging, a five-day lift ticket or Nordic trail package, a mountain tour, a ski race, a welcome party, and discount coupons for shopping in the towns of Sun Valley and Ketcham. A big-band dinner dance is optional.

Schweitzer Mountain's Prime Timers Club for skiers 55 and over is an informal club whose members ski together almost every day and get together for social gatherings every Thursday afternoon. In addition, there's a bargain senior ski week in March, the Snowmaster's Classic, a week of workshops, clinics, social activities, and race training for older skiers who are seeking to improve their technical abilities.

MAINE

At Sunday River Ski Resort, those who purchase the Perfect Turn Gold Card or Platinum Card and are 50 or over are eligible for unlimited membership in the Prime Time Club. The club skis together with an instructor for two hours every Saturday and Sunday morning. The cards also entitle participants to discounts on private ski clinics.

At Sugarloaf/USA, a Perfect Turn Platinum Card is what you need to participate in the Prime Time Club for skiers over 50. At this ski area, the senior clinic meets for lessons on Tuesday and Thursday afternoons.

MASSACHUSETTS

Jiminy Peak in Hancock holds Senior Day every Thursday, when, if you already have a season pass or are over 70, the cost is only $20 for a lift ticket and a two-hour ski clinic. For others, the day costs twice as much.

At Catamount, members of the 70+ Club ski for $7 any time.

MICHIGAN

At Crystal Mountain Resort, every Tuesday is Silver Streak Day, and skiers over the age of 55 are entitled to free group lessons. At Caberfae Peaks, Silver Streak Day is on Thursdays, and you may ski all day for $12 if you are over 50. And, if you are over 55, check out Senior Week, held every January at Sugar Loaf Resort. You'll get half-price skiing, a good deal on accommodations, and free NASTAR.

NEVADA

At Mt. Rose, just outside of Reno, skiers over 50 are welcomed every Friday morning for coffee and a free two-hour mountain clinic with senior instructors.

NEW HAMPSHIRE

It's a rare ski area in this state that does not offer older skiers an impressive break on lift tickets at age 65 or so and a free pass at 70. Many also have special programs for senior skiers.

At Waterville Valley, Silver Streaks, for skiers over 55, offers reserved parking, coffee and pastries in the base lodge, free overnight ski check, and a guided warmup run. Members also receive special instructional clinics throughout the season. Cost is a daily fee of $2 or a season pass for $50. Silver Streaks also meets at the Nordic Center for cross-country skiers.

At Attitash Bear Peak, TGIF (Thank Goodness I'm Fifty) meets Thursdays for a ski clinic that includes instruction, fitness workshops, races, and a party.

At Loon Mountain, Flying 50s Plus meets every Thursday and Friday morning except on holidays for two-hour group skiing. Members also get discounts on lift tickets, lodging, and special activities.

At Cannon Mountain, Senior Cruises, for skiers over 50, meets Monday mornings to ski for two hours with instructors.

At Gunstock, Mountain Meisters, for over-50 skiers, meets every Thursday for skills clinics and video analysis. Special events include a recreational race day.

At Temple Mountain, the Morning Birds, a seven-week program for seniors, runs Monday through Friday with lessons on skiing or snowboarding.

At King Pine at Purity Spring Resort, for five days in January skiers over 50 get free lessons in alpine or cross-country skiing or snowboarding. Reservations are required.

NEW MEXICO

What senior skiers get almost everywhere in New Mexico are reduced fees for lift tickets at 62 or 65 and, in some areas, free skiing at 70. And at Taos Ski Valley, in the Sangre de Cristo Mountains, the Masters Ski Week gives 50-plus skiers group lessons, lift tickets, video analysis, races, and social events.

NEW YORK

Skiers over 50 are invited to join the Ski Windham Senior Skier Development Program for eight weeks on Tuesdays from January to March. You may attend the program by the day, if you prefer. What you get is morning coffee, presentations on ski-related subjects, morning and afternoon lessons, lunch, and workshops.

PENNSYLVANIA

At Blue Knob Four Seasons Resort in Claysburg, skiers over 65 pay junior rates any time, and those over 70 ski free mid-week.

UTAH

Virtually all of Utah's ski areas give senior skiers reduced rates on lift tickets at 60 or 65, with Sundance and Elk Meadows offering free rides to those over 65. Most others stop charging at 70—except Alta, where you must wait until you are 80!

At Snowbird, join Junior's Seniors, a complimentary program for advanced senior skiers over 62 every Tuesday morning. Come back in the afternoon and pay a nominal fee for three more hours of skiing with Junior Bounous. Another program, Silverwings, is offered at Snowbird, this one for experienced skiers over the age of 50, with full-day classes on Wednesdays and Thursdays.

Alta's ski school gives special three-hour Silver Meisters lessons on Fridays and Sundays designed specifically for mature skiers who want to improve their skills.

The seniors program at Sundance sets aside four afternoon sessions a month for group skiing with a guide.

As for Brighton Ski Resort, the Senior Workshop, held on three consecutive weeks for skiers of all levels over 50, includes lessons, a lift pass, breakfast, and a social hour.

VERMONT

Vermont's ski areas were the first to cater to older skiers, and it is highly unlikely that there are any resorts there that don't give seniors a decent break on lift tickets and season passes. Along with special rates, several areas offer special senior programs as well. Here's a sample.

At Jay Peak any skier over the age of 55 is invited to join the Silver Peaks Club, a group that skis together every Tuesday. For a nominal fee, you are entitled to a day on the slopes, guided tours, coffee and doughnuts, and après-ski activities. If you're over 65, you may ski here any time for $10 a day.

The It'SnoWonder is a club for skiers over 55 at Smuggler's Notch, offering its members skiing every Wednesday, plus coffee and doughnuts, half-price rental equipment and group ski lessons, 50 percent off day ticket rates, mountain tours, videotaped skiing, afternoon get-togethers with speakers, discussions, and a farewell barbecue. Membership fee is $10 for the season.

The Silver Griffins Senior Program at Bromley Mountain meets every nonholiday Monday and Tuesday for group skiing, fun races, picnics, and parties. Members of the group get preferred parking midweek and discounts on food, equipment, and lessons.

15

Back to Summer Camp

Maybe you thought camp was just for kids, but if you are a grown-up person who likes the outdoors, swimming, boating, birds, and arts and crafts and appreciates fields and forests and star-filled skies, you too can pack your bags and go off on a sleepaway. Throughout the country, many camps set aside weeks for adult sessions, while others offer adult programs all season long. More and more adults are getting hooked on summer camp, and many wouldn't miss a year.

ELDERHOSTEL
Many of Elderhostel's programs are a combination of camping and college. In this wildly successful low-cost educational program (see Chapter 16 for details), you can spend a week or two camping in remote scenic areas, enjoying all the activities from horseback riding to crafts, boating,

campfires, and sleeping in a cabin or under the stars.
For information: Elderhostel, 75 Federal St., Boston, MA
02110; 617-426-7788. In Canada: Elderhostel Canada, 5
Cataraqui St., Kingston, ON K7K 1Z7; 613-530-2222.

RV ELDERHOSTELS

Less expensive than regular Elderhostel programs because
you take along your own housing, these programs come in
two varieties. One is the usual Elderhostel educational vacation on a college campus, where you partake of the happenings, including courses, meals, and excursions, with the
rest of the group but sleep in your own RV, trailer, or tent
on the campus or at nearby campgrounds. The other is a
mobile program or moving field trip—in Alaska, for example, Wyoming, the Yukon, or along the Oregon Trail—where
you'll hear the lectures over your CB radio as you travel.
Moving along like a wagon train, you travel in a group led
by an experienced guide and make many stops for lectures
and sight-seeing as you go.
For information: Elderhostel, 75 Federal St., Boston, MA
02110; 617-426-7788. In Canada: Elderhostel Canada, 5
Cataraqui St., Kingston, ON K7K 1Z7; 613-530-2222.

GRANDPARENTS/GRANDCHILDREN CAMP
See Chapter 3 for information about summer camps and
other vacations designed to give grandparents and grandchildren some special time together.

THE SALVATION ARMY
The Salvation Army operates scores of rural camps across
the country, most of which have year-round adult sessions.

The camps are run by regional divisional headquarters of the Army; thus each is different from the others. Open to anyone, they cost very little.

For information: Contact a local unit of the Salvation Army.

VOLUNTARY ASSOCIATION FOR SENIOR CITIZEN ACTIVITIES

VASCA is a nonprofit organization that will provide you with detailed information about camps in the New York area for people over the age of 55. The agency represents 11 vacation lodges scattered about New York, New Jersey, Connecticut, and Pennsylvania, all of them amazingly affordable. Some are small rustic country retreats, most are lakeside resorts, others are huge sprawling complexes with endless activities. Several are designed to accommodate the disabled and the blind as well as the very elderly. The camps are sponsored by various nonprofit organizations and foundations, some with religious affiliations but nonsectarian.

For information: VASCA, 281 Park Ave. South, New York, NY 10010; 212-645-6590.

YMCA/YWCA

The Y runs many camps, most of them for children, but some also offer inexpensive weeks for adults. For example, the YMCA of the Rockies operates a resort, Snow Mountain Ranch, with a special program in mid-August for active adults over the age of 50 at its Camp Chief Ouray in Granby, Colorado. The High Point YMCA's Camp Cheerio in the Appalachian Mountains of North Carolina sets aside three weeks a year for campers over 50, who live in the same cabins and pursue the same activities as the kids do the rest of the summer.

For information: Call your local YMCA or YWCA for information about camps in your area.

CAMPS SPONSORED BY CHURCH GROUPS

There are many adult camps and summer workshops sponsored by religious organizations, too many and too diverse to list here. One source of information is Christian Camping International, which sells a guide listing about 850 camps and conferences in the U.S.

For information: Christian Camping International/USA, PO Box 62189, Colorado Springs, CO 80962; 719-260-9400.

AUDUBON ECOLOGY CAMPS

Not for over-50s alone, these are included here because mature nature lovers will enjoy these natural-history programs for adults run by the National Audubon Society. There are three Audubon Ecology Camps for grown-ups (in Wyoming, Maine, and Connecticut) where the outdoors is used as a classroom for six-day sessions during the summer months. Here you live on-site while you learn all about the surrounding environment, from marine and island ecology to mountain, meadow, woods, and water habitats.

For information: National Audubon Society, 613 Riversville Rd., Greenwich, CT 06831; 203-869-2017.

16

Going Back to School After 50

Have you always wanted to learn French, study African birds, examine Eskimo culture, learn to paddle a canoe or ski down a mountain, delve into archaeology, international finance, horticulture, the language of whales, or great literature of the 19th century? Now is the time to do it. If you're a typical member of the over-50 generation, you're in good shape, healthy and alert, with the energy and the time to pursue new interests. So why not go back to school and learn all those things you've always wished you knew?

You are welcome as a regular student at just about any institution in the United States and Canada, especially in the continuing-education programs, but many colleges and universities have set up special programs designed to lure older people back to the classroom. Some offer good reductions in tuition (so good indeed that often you may attend regular classes at half price or even free) and give credits for life experience. Others have designed programs, and sometimes whole schools, specifically for mature scholars.

Going back to class is an excellent way to generate feelings of accomplishment and to exercise the mind—and one of the best ways to make new friends. It doesn't necessarily mean you'll have to turn in term papers or take excruciatingly difficult exams. Sign up for one class a week on flower arranging or Spanish conversation or a once-a-month lecture series on managing your money. Or register as a part-time or full-time student in a traditional university program. Or take a learning vacation on a college campus. Do it *your* way.

You don't even have to attend classes to learn on vacation. You can go on archaeological digs, count butterflies, help save turtles from extinction, brush up on your bassoon playing, listen to opera, search for Roman remains in Europe, study dancing or French cuisine, or go on safari in Africa.

EDUCATIONAL TRAVEL PROGRAMS
CHAUTAUQUA INSTITUTION

For over a century people have been traveling up to the shores of Lake Chautauqua, in southwestern New York State, to a cultural summer center set in a Victorian village. The 856-acre hilltop complex offers a wide variety of educational programs, including summer weeks and off-season weekends designed for people over the age of 55. The 55-Plus Weekends and the Residential Week for Older Adults are filled up far in advance, so if you are interested, don't waste a moment before signing up.

Each 55-Plus Weekend has a specific focus, such as the U.S. Constitution, natural history, national politics, music appreciation, or trade relations with Japan. They include discussions, workshops, lectures, films, recreational activities, and evening entertainment, all led by professionals. Housing and meals are available in a residence hall with double rooms and shared baths.

The Residential Week for Older Adults is similar but longer. And it includes lodging and meals as well as admittance to other happenings at the center.

It's all quite cheap. The cost of tuition, room, meals, and planned activities for a Residential Week is currently $425, while a 55-Plus Weekend costs $30 for commuters or $125 if you want accommodations and meals.

For information: Program Center for Older Adults, Chautauqua, NY 14722; 800-836-ARTS or 716-357-6200.

A WEEK IN THE MOUNTAINS

Explore is a learning vacation in early fall for "active mature adults" over the age of 50. Set in Beaver Creek, in Vail Valley, Colorado, it offers symposia, hands-on workshops, guest speakers, and outdoor recreational clinics mixed with social activities and exercise. The sessions focus on a choice of topics from global political issues to art, history, music appreciation, and astronomy. Workshops may include such subjects as wildlife photography, painting, and gourmet cooking, while the outdoor clinics range from fly fishing to fitness walking.

For information: Explore, NorthStar Institute, 312 S. Franklin St., Denver, CO 80209; 800-298-4242 or 303-777-6873.

CLOSE UP FOUNDATION

Close Up, in cooperation with AARP, invites thousands of older Americans to Washington, D.C., in the spring and fall, when the temperature is just right, for an insider's view of the government at work. Its goal is to help participants become more informed about current events, exchange views with political insiders and national leaders, attend exclusive seminars featuring public-policy experts, and take part in workshops designed to illustrate how public policy affects them and how they can affect it.

You'll spend extensive time on Capitol Hill, visit a foreign embassy, take study tours of monuments and museums, go to the theater, attend dinners, lodge in a comfortable hotel, and have some free time as well. Moderately priced (currently $680 to $1,230, depending on the events), programs range from five days to a week and include everything: lodging, meals, all activities and excursions. Programs are available to both individuals and groups.

About a dozen programs are offered every year in the spring and fall by this nonprofit nonpartisan organization that has now brought over 480,000 people of all ages to the capital city. Some of the programs emphasize history and take you to Colonial Williamsburg and Jamestown; others target the presidency and show you the presidential homesteads; but the main focus always remains "inside" Washington.

The Congressional Senior Citizen Intern Program, developed by Close Up, is another way to get a firsthand look at the government. You may apply to be an intern and, if accepted, spend a few days working with the congressional

staff in the office of your own representative or senator.
For information: Close Up Foundation, 44 Canal Center Plaza, Alexandria, VA 22314; 800-363-4762 or 703-706-3668.

THE COLLEGE AT 60

Part of Fordham University and located at the Lincoln Center campus in New York City, the College at 60 offers credit courses in liberal arts subjects such as history, psychology, philosophy, economics, literature, music, art, and computers, taught by Fordham faculty members. Included are a lecture series and the use of all college facilities. After taking four seminars, students receive a certificate and are encouraged to enter the regular Fordham University program. Courses may be audited or taken for credit for fees that are half of the regular rates.

Believe it or not, you are eligible for the College at 60 when you are 50.

For information: The College at 60, Fordham University at Lincoln Center, 113 W. 60th St., Room 804, New York, NY 10023; 212-636-6740.

ELDERFOLK

Each of Elderfolk's two- to five-week courses in Nepal, India, Tibet, Bhutan, China, and Pakistan focuses on Himalayan culture, history, natural history, religion, native cuisine, and arts and crafts. Exclusively for adventurers over the age of 55, they are offered by the Folkways Institute, a small international school without walls "whose projects are designed to permit cross-cultural understanding," which plans study courses for students and professors.

Some of the courses, combining education and exotic travel, are cultural treks on which you'll be put up at night in roomy tents or lodges. Others are residential or overland trips where you lodge in small hotels or guest houses, such as the Ancient Silk Road trip from Xian to Lahore.

No expertise or training is required, but some stamina definitely is.

For information: Elderfolk, Folkways Institute, 14600 SE Aldridge Rd., Portland, OR 97236-6518; 800-225-4666 or 503-658-6600.

ELDERHOSTEL

Elderhostel, the educational travel program for mature people, offers some of the world's best bargains. Astonishingly inexpensive and infinitely varied, Elderhostel's short-term academic programs number in the thousands. They are hosted by over 2,000 educational and cultural institutions in every U.S. state and Canadian province as well as 70 foreign countries. The idea is to sign up for a program in a place you want to visit that offers courses you want to take. The only requirement for participation is that you must be 55 or over. An accompanying spouse or companion may be any age.

Started in the mid-70s as a way for colleges to make use of their idle facilities, empty dorms, and teaching talent during summer vacations, Elderhostel programs are now offered all year. The organization acts as a clearinghouse for the host institutions, each of which designs its own programs that include three academic classes taught by the faculty and may use the Elderhostel name if they meet certain criteria.

On domestic Elderhostels, the programs usually start on a Sunday afternoon and last five or six nights. The typical cost is around $350, including accommodations, meals, five days of classes, and a variety of extracurricular activities. Foreign trips, more expensive, include airfare and are two to four weeks long. In most cases, you'll lodge on college or university campuses and enjoy the cultural and recreational resources that go with them. You'll take three courses taught by the faculty, but there are no exams, grades, or homework, nor do you get college credits for them. The accommodations are plain but comfortable, the food institutional but nourishing. There are usually two twin beds to a room, with a bathroom down the hall. And there is no maid service. On the other hand, the setting is often beautiful, the courses interesting, and the company remarkably varied.

The course offerings are myriad. Look through the voluminous catalogs published every season for state-by-state and country-by-country listings of host institutions and the classes they offer. Or view them on the Internet or at your public library.

HOSTELSHIPS

Elderhostel offers a limited number of full or partial scholarships, to be used only in the U.S., for people who find the tuition costs of the programs beyond their means. Funds to cover travel costs are not included and eligibility is determined upon completion of an application that includes a confidential questionnaire. Scholarship programs in Alaska and Hawaii are available only to residents of these states.
For information: Write to Elderhostel, 75 Federal St., Boston MA 02110. Attention: Hostelships.

Some of the domestic programs include sports and adventures, from canoeing to skiing, hiking, biking, and more. Overseas, there are walking trips in Switzerland and bike trips in such places as Austria, Denmark, England, France, and the Netherlands (see Chapter 13). And a Homestay program lets you live with a foreign family for one week out of a two-week trip (see Chapter 11).

If you'd like to contribute your time, energy, and expertise to a volunteer organization that provides significant services all over the world, look into the Elderhostel Service Program (see Chapter 18). Elderhostel has joined forces with scores of national nonprofit organizations to create service opportunities for people over 55.

If you want to take your adult children or grandchildren along, you'll find intergenerational programs as well (see Chapter 3).

There is sure to be a program somewhere in a place you've always wanted to visit, giving courses you've always wanted to take, at any time of the year. In Quebec Province in Canada, you can take your classes in French. Ask to be placed on the mailing list for the seasonal catalogs.

For information: Elderhostel, 75 Federal St., Boston, MA 02110; 617-426-7788. In Canada: Elderhostel Canada, 5 Cataraqui St., Kingston, ON K7K 1Z7; 613-530-2222.

ELDERTREKS

The exotic adventures planned by ElderTreks to places such as China, Nepal, Tibet, Thailand, Vietnam, and Borneo qualify as travel/study trips because they immerse you in the cultures you visit. See Chapter 5 for more.

For information: ElderTreks, 597 Markham St., Toronto, ON M6G 2L7; 800-741-7956 or 416-588-5000.

INTERHOSTEL

An international study/travel program for energetic people over the age of 50 (a companion need be only 40), Interhostel is sponsored by the University of New Hampshire. It offers more than 75 two-week learning vacations each year around the world, from Africa to Europe, Australia, New Zealand, Asia, the French West Indies, Mexico, Costa Rica, and South America, about which its three free catalogs a year will keep you posted. The idea is to stay in one country long enough to become well acquainted with the place you are visiting. During your stay, you will be introduced to the history, culture, and people through lectures, field trips, sight-seeing excursions, and social and cultural activities. Your group, from 25 to 40 participants, will be accompanied by a representative of the university. Trips are scheduled year-round and are cosponsored by educational institutions in the host countries.

Living quarters, clean and comfortable although not necessarily fancy, are in residence halls or modest hotels. Most meals are cafeteria-style and feature the local food of the region. The cost, moderate for what you get, includes full room and board, tuition, airfare, and ground transportation.

Because Interhostel's adventures impose a busy schedule of activities, you should be healthy and fit, full of vim and vigor, able to climb stairs, tote your own baggage, and walk comfortably at a moderate pace for more than a mile

at a time. This is especially important if you join one of Interhostel's new walking programs (see Chapter 13).

For information: Interhostel, University of New Hampshire, 6 Garrison Ave., Durham, NH 03824; 800-733-9753
or 603-862-1147.

NATIONAL ACADEMY OF OLDER CANADIANS

Based in Vancouver, the NAOC's mission is to involve older
Canadians in lifelong learning and to work in partnership
with other nonprofit organizations to develop programs to
promote its membership's contribution to society. These
programs currently include computer classes, business
training, workshops, learning circles, mentoring, town
meetings, and discussion groups on issues of special interest. Annual membership fee is $20.

For information: National Academy of Older Canadians,
411 Dunsmuir St., Vancouver, BC V6B 1X4; 604-681-3767.

NORTH CAROLINA CENTER FOR CREATIVE RETIREMENT

The NCCR involves more than 1,500 50-plus participants
every year in its five-component program: the College for
Seniors, in which members teach and learn together; a lead-
ership for seniors program, which explores the history, civic
life, and challenges of the community; an intergenerational
mentoring program that matches retirees with university
undergraduates; community volunteering; and a retirement
relocation weekend program that covers everything from
housing options to hiking trails in western North Carolina.

For information: The North Carolina Center for Creative

Retirement, 116 Rhodes Hall, University of North Carolina at Asheville, Asheville, NC 28804; 704-251-6140.

OASIS

OASIS (Older Adult Service and Information System) is a nonprofit organization sponsored by the May Department Stores Company in collaboration with local hospitals, medical centers, government agencies, and other participants in about 44 locations in 26 cities across the nation. Its purpose is to enrich the lives of people over 55 by providing educational and wellness programs and volunteer opportunities to its members. At its centers, OASIS offers classes ranging from French conversation and the visual arts to dance, bridge, creative writing, history, exercise, classical music, points of law, and prevention of osteoporosis. Also featured are special events such as concerts, plays, and museum exhibits; lectures; and even trips and cruises. If you live in an OASIS city, sign up—this is a good deal. Membership is free.

For information: The OASIS Institute, 7710 Carondelet Ave., Ste. 125, St. Louis, MO 63105; 314-862-2933.

PLUS PROGRAM, NYU

All students over 65 who register for at least one regular course for which they pay half tuition in the School of Continuing Education at New York University are eligible to become members of PLUS, a Program of Lifelong Learning for University Seniors, for an additional fee of $75 per semester. Membership includes a choice of two specially designed, five-session mini-courses on a broad range of subjects. Topics for the courses, scheduled on Monday, Tuesday, and Thursday afternoons, have recently included Great Decisions in Foreign Policy, Archaeology of New York City, and the Genius of George Gershwin. PLUS members may also attend five weekly luncheon/discussion lectures with prominent speakers.

For information: PLUS, NYU School of Continuing Education, 11 W. 42nd St., New York, NY 10036; 212-790-1352 or 212-998-7130.

SAGA HOLIDAYS

Saga Holidays, marketing travel only for people over 50, offers travel/study programs as well as myriad escorted tours and cruises. One is its own series of Smithsonian Odyssey Tours and another is the Road Scholar program, with itineraries that feature educational themes. The programs include expert lecturers, selected literature, and predeparture educational materials. See Chapter 5 for more.

For information: Saga Holidays, 222 Berkeley St., Boston, MA 02116; 800-343-0273; Smithsonian Odyssey tours: 800-258-5885. Road Scholar program: 800-621-2151.

SEMESTER AT SEA

A 100-day educational voyage around the world, Semester at Sea, sponsored by the University of Pittsburgh and the Institute for Shipboard Education, takes over 500 college students and 50 to 60 "senior scholars" on a unique learning experience designed to advance the exchange of understanding and knowledge between cultures. The S.S. *Universe Explorer*, a former cruise ship refitted as a floating campus, circumnavigates the earth twice a year, visiting countries of the non-Western world that have included Japan, China, India, Malaysia, Kenya, Brazil, Venezuela,

Egypt, Israel, South Africa, Greece, Turkey, Vietnam, and Morocco.

While the college students earn credit hours toward an undergraduate degree, the older participants may audit classes or enroll for full credit, choosing from among 60 courses taught by faculty from various universities. On-board courses range from anthropology and biological sciences to economics, fine arts, philosophy, political science, and religion. Lengthy stays in each port of call give students a chance to experience the peoples and cultures firsthand.

Amenities include an adult coordinator, entertainment, buffet-style meals, lectures, discussion groups, guest scholars with expertise in local cultures, films, art shows, sports, and more.

For information: Semester at Sea, 811 William Pitt Union, University of Pittsburgh, Pittsburgh, PA 15260; 800-854-0195 or 412-648-7490.

SENIOR SUMMER SCHOOL

Here's your chance to sample college life and take courses for 2 to 10 weeks in the summer with lodging in private or university residential halls. Senior Summer School is a consortium of six colleges and universities: the University of Wisconsin, the University of California at Santa Barbara, San Diego State University, the University of Maine in Bangor, the University of Judaism in Los Angeles, and Mt. Allison University in New Brunswick, Canada. Courses are college level, but there are no marks, grades, compulsory papers, or mandatory attendance requirements. Included in the programs are all meals, weekly housekeeping, excursions, and social activities. A mix of couples and singles, senior students include those who never finished high school as well as those with college and postgraduate degrees. *For information:* Senior Summer School, PO Box 4424, Deerfield Beach, FL 33442; 800-847-2466.

SENIOR VENTURES

Southern Oregon University in Ashland, a town famed for its annual Oregon Shakespeare Festival, offers educational theater programs with classes taught by actors and backstage professionals, plus theater tickets and museum admissions. Meals, lodging on campus, and transportation between the airport and the campus are included. Senior

LEARNING COMPUTER TECHNOLOGY

SeniorNet is a national nonprofit organization dedicated to building a community of computer-literate older adults, providing them with information and instruction about computer technologies. It sponsors 115 SeniorNet Learning Centers, staffed by volunteers, around the U.S. where members may take classes and use the facilities. Independent members participate through the organization's electronic community, SeniorNet Online.

Membership costs $35 ($40 for couples) for the first year and $25 (or $30) after that. Among its benefits are a quarterly newsletter, discounts on computer-related materials, and the opportunity to meet other members and build friendships online and, at biannual conferences, in person.

SeniorNet maintains two websites, one on the Internet and the other on AOL. Internet: www.seniornet.org. AOL: seniornet.

For information: SeniorNet, 1 Kearny St., San Francisco, CA 94108; 800-747-6848. E-mail: seniornet@aol.com.

Ventures also presents residential bridge-and-theater courses and a few travel adventures, including a 10-day tour of the Texas hill country and a Canadian theater expedition. *For information:* Senior Ventures, Southern Oregon University, 1250 Siskiyou Blvd., Ashland, OR 97520; 800-257-0577 or 541-552-6285.

TRAVELEARN

The upscale learning vacations by TraveLearn take small groups of adults all over the world, putting you up in first-class or deluxe accommodations and providing faculty escorts chosen from a nationwide network of more than 280 cooperating universities and colleges, as well as local lecturers, in each place you visit. You'll learn through on-site lectures, seminars, meals with local families, visits to homes and workplaces, and field trips. Destinations include Ireland, Egypt, Kenya, Indonesia, China, Morocco, Greece, Israel, Italy, Turkey, South Africa, Costa Rica, and more. If you are traveling alone and wish to share a room with another single traveler, you are guaranteed the double rate if you register 90 days in advance, even if a roommate is not found for you.

For information: TraveLearn, PO Box 315, Lakeville, PA 18438; 717-226-9114.

UNIVERSITY VACATIONS

Spend a week or more at a famous university in Europe, concentrating on a choice of subjects from the legend of Camelot to the works of Jane Austen, Roman Britain, modern mystery writers, English operetta, radio astronomy, and the American Colonies. You'll stay on campus or in a first-class hotel and attend lectures presented by university scholars, go on excursions to relevant locations, eat full breakfasts and four-course dinners. The participating universities include Oxford and Cambridge, in England; the University of Bologna, in Italy; the University of Leiden, in the Netherlands; Charles University, in Prague; the University of Paris-Sorbonne; Pontifical Gregorian University, in Rome; and Harvard University, in Boston. Open to all ages, especially yours.

For information: University Vacations, 3660 Bougainvillea Rd., Coconut Grove, FL 33133; 800-792-0100 or 305-567-2904.

INSTITUTES FOR LEARNING IN RETIREMENT

Today there are about 230 community-based Institutes for Learning in Retirement throughout the U.S. and Canada that provide noncredit college-level courses for adults of retirement age who are local people who commute to the programs. Each institute is sponsored by a college or university as a center for intellectual and social activity for its participants who are involved in determining curriculum, recruiting new members, and developing academic and social programs. Most ILRs are governed by their own members and have members leading some of the academic course work.

In most cases, there are no tests or grades, although there may be assigned reading or other preparation. Students pay a modest annual membership fee and may usually take as many courses as they wish. At some institutions, they may take some regular undergraduate or adult education courses as well. Membership is open to everyone, and no previous level of education is required.

For a list of learning programs and/or information about starting a new program, contact the Elderhostel Institute Network, an association of independent ILRs whose purpose is to support established ILRs and extend the concept to new communities.

For information: Elderhostel Institute Network, 75 Federal St., Boston, MA 02110; 617-422-0784.

17

Shopping Breaks, Taxes, Insurance, and Other Practical Matters

I n this chapter you won't find suggestions for interesting vacation possibilities, or unusual places to explore. Instead, its purpose is to provide useful information about benefits and services that could be coming to you simply because you are now sufficiently mature to take advantage of them.

SAVE MONEY IN THE STORES

All over the U.S. and Canada, retail stores now offer discounts to seniors because they realize that members of the mature crowd are cautious consumers who know the value of a dollar, are extremely fond of bargains, and have the potential of becoming loyal customers. In fact, the older population has now started to expect reduced prices when they shop.

Stores vary on the age you must be to receive their special offers, but most start you off at 60. Some give you 10 or 15 percent off every day, while others reserve one day a week for their senior discounts. Sometimes, however, instead of discounts, they advertise senior specials. Sears and Montgomery Ward, on the other hand, have clubs to join that entitle you to special discounts and other services.

MONTGOMERY WARD

Montgomery Ward's Y.E.S. (Years of Extra Savings) Discount Club saves you money in many ways when you've reached the age of 55. As a member, you receive a membership card and a bimonthly magazine called *Vantage*. The membership fee is currently $3.49 per month or $34.99 a year for you and your spouse. With the membership card in hand, you will get 10 percent off any merchandise, sale or nonsale, in all Montgomery Ward stores every Tuesday. On Tuesdays, Wednesdays, and Thursdays, you're entitled to 10 percent off any auto labor charges. And there are other benefits, such as a pharmaceutical service.

What's more, the Y.E.S. Club Travel Service plans your travel, makes reservations, and gives you discounted prices plus cash rebates on the cost of your trips. This means that upon your return you will receive a check for a 10 percent rebate on all lodging and car rentals, and 5 percent on tours, cruises, rail passes, and airline tickets.

For information: Montgomery Ward Y.E.S. Discount Club, 200 N. Martingale Rd., Schaumburg, IL 60173; 800-421-5396.

SEARS

Sears started Mature Outlook many years ago for its over-50 customers. Among the club's benefits are savings to members when they cash in special discount coupons good for a variety of products and services. The coupons are included in the club magazine and may be used in all Sears stores in the U.S. and Canada. See Chapter 19 for more about Mature Outlook.

For information: Mature Outlook, PO Box 10448, Des Moines, IA 50306-0448; 800-336-6330.

FEDERAL INCOME TAXES

The tax laws no longer provide an extra exemption for people over the age of 65. Instead, they give you a larger standard deduction than younger people are entitled to, according to Julian Block, tax attorney and author of a popular guide to saving on income taxes, *Julian Block's Tax Avoidance Secrets.*

The standard deductions for everyone under 65 for 1998 returns are $7,100 for married couples filing jointly; $3,550 each for married people filing separately; $4,250 for single people; and $6,250 for heads of households. These standard deductions change every year to reflect inflation, so be sure to check them out for each year's return.

If one spouse of a couple filing jointly is over 65, the standard deduction is increased for 1998 returns (by $850) to $7,950. If both members of a married couple are over 65, it is increased (by $850 twice) to $8,800.

For a married person over 65 filing separately, the

deduction increases (by $850) to $4,400. A single person over 65 may deduct $5,300 ($1,050 more than those who are younger). And a head of household over 65 gets a standard deduction in 1998 of $7,300 ($1,050 more than an under-65).

None of these figures apply, of course, if you itemize your deductions. Remember that at age 65 you needn't file returns at all when your reportable income is below the amount required for filing.

By the way, the Internal Revenue Service issues a free booklet, *Tax Information for Older Americans* (Publication No. 554), which you can get at your local IRS office or by calling 800-TAX-FORM. You may also want to ask for its free *Guide to Free Tax Services* (Publication No. 910), which provides a list of IRS booklets on federal taxes and explains what each one covers. Request large-print tax forms if you need them.

HOW TO GET HELP
WITH YOUR TAX RETURN

Assistance in preparing your tax returns is available free from both the Internal Revenue Service and AARP. The IRS offers Tax Counseling for the Elderly (TCE) for people over 60 and Voluntary Income Tax Assistants (VITA) for younger people who need help. Trained volunteers provide information and will prepare returns at thousands of sites throughout the country from February 2 to April 15. Watch your local newspaper for a list of sites in your area or call 800-TAX-1040 and press 0.

Or you may enlist the help of AARP's Tax-Aide Service at more than 10,000 sites nationwide where, in the 10-week period before April 15, volunteers help low- and moderate-income members of AARP to prepare their tax returns. Volunteers will even go to your home, when necessary, if you are physically unable to get to a site. To find the site nearest you, call 888-AARP-NOW (800-227-7669). Or call your regional or state AARP offices. Have your membership number and zip code handy and also your calendar, as an appointment is required.

SAVE ON AUTO AND HOMEOWNER'S INSURANCE

Mature people tend to be cautious drivers, much more careful than the younger crowd, having shed their bad habits such as speeding and reckless driving. And, although older drivers total more accidents per mile, they drive fewer miles, usually don't use their cars for daily commuting, and tend to stay off the roads at night and in bad weather. Therefore, statistically, they have fewer accidents per driver than other risk categories do, at least until they are over the age of 75. Because of lower claims costs, insurance companies often offer discounts on automobile coverage after a certain age, in most cases 55, sometimes raising them again after age 70 or 75.

In addition, you may get a discount—usually 10 percent—on some of your automobile coverage in most states when you successfully complete a state-approved defensive-driving course. Among the programs is AARP's 55 Alive/Mature Driving, an eight-hour classroom refresher that specifically addresses the needs of older drivers with physical and perceptual changes that affect their driving.

Open to both AARP members and nonmembers at a current cost of $8 per person, and taught by volunteers, the course is offered locally all over the country. Defensive-driving courses are also offered by other groups, including local high schools and the AAA.

Some companies also offer reductions in premiums for homeowner's insurance, figuring you have become a cautious, reliable sort who not only takes good care of your property but is likely to spend more time at home these days keeping your eye on things.

Although discounts are wonderful and we all love to get them, always shop the bottom line when you buy insurance; in other words, know what you are getting for what you are paying. Rates for the same coverage can differ by hundreds of dollars, so you must be a comparison shopper to get the best deal for you. If one company charges higher premiums for comparable coverage and then gives you a discount, you have not profited.

Insurance regulations differ from state to state, but here are some of the offerings made in some states to older drivers and homeowners by some major insurance companies.

ALLSTATE

Allstate gives a discount of 10 percent off the premiums across the board—liability, comprehensive, and collision coverage—on automobile insurance in almost every state for those who are 55 and retired. And, in over 30 states, it takes an additional 5 or 10 percent off for graduates of an approved defensive-driving course. In Florida, things can get even better. Here drivers age 50 to 70 may apply for an additional 3 to 7 percent discount on top of the others.

As for property coverage, Allstate offers 10 percent off the premiums in most states to homeowners at age 55, 10 percent to renters, and 5 percent to condominium owners who are retired.

HOW TO SAVE YOUR LIFE

If you get sick or have an accident away from home, a non-profit foundation called **MedicAlert** may save your health or even your life. For an initial fee of $35 and $15 a year thereafter, you receive a stainless-steel bracelet or neck chain engraved with your personal identification number, a 24-hour-a-day toll-free telephone number, and a brief description of your medical condition. Information about your treatment is kept on file and is available by telephone to you or medical personnel who may need it in an emergency. Included are names and telephone numbers of your physicians and those to notify if necessary. As a backup, you get a wallet card with the same information printed on it.
For information: MedicAlert Foundation, PO Box 1009, Turlock, CA 95381; 800-344-3226.

AMERICAN FAMILY

If you are between the ages of 50 and 69, American Family gives you 10 percent off on almost all auto coverages. Preferred customers—those with good driving records—who buy both auto and homeowner insurance from this company get another discount of about 10 percent. Not only that, but taking a defensive-driving course nets you an additional 5 to 10 percent discount in some states.

COLONIAL PENN

With this insurance company, you can save up to 10 percent on your automobile coverage in most states if you are 55 or over and retired. Take a defensive-driving course and you'll save 10 percent more. You are guaranteed to get a policy renewal, regardless of your age or driving record, as long as you meet a few simple requirements, such as paying your premiums and maintaining a valid driver's license.

FARMERS

Policyholders over the age of 50 or 55 are offered discounts of 7 to 15 percent on automobile coverage in most states where Farmers Insurance is sold if they complete an approved defensive-driving course. A homeowner's credit starts at age 50 and ranges from 2 to 10 percent, depending on your age and the state in which you reside.

GEICO

In most states and for most driving situations, GEICO offers good drivers between the ages of 50 and 74, retired or not, a lower rate on all automobile coverages on the cars they principally operate that are not used for business. A certificate from a qualifying driving course gives an additional 10 percent discount for the next three years for all drivers 50 and over.

In addition, a Prime Time contract is available in many states. To be eligible for it, the principal operator of the household must be over 50, no one on the policy may be under 25, and no drivers may have had an accident or driving conviction within the last three years. But, once issued, the company guarantees to continue to renew your policy, subject to certain conditions, regardless of your age, accidents, or driving convictions.

THE HARTFORD

The automobile and homeowner insurance offered by AARP is underwritten by The Hartford and gives you a 5 percent discount for maintaining a safe driving record for three years, 10 percent after another three years, and an additional 10 percent discount for the next three years when you complete an accredited driving course. Policies are issued for 12 months, locking in your rate for a year, and may not be cancelled because of age or accident record.

Policyholders also get full value replacement cost coverage; in other words, if an insured new vehicle is declared a total loss within the first six months after purchase or up to 7,500 miles, whichever is first, it will be replaced with an identical new car or you will be reimbursed for its cost without deduction for depreciation.

As for homeowner insurance, in most states The Hartford gives discounts of up to 5 percent on the total premium at any age if you and your spouse are retired or work fewer than 24 hours a week.

NATIONWIDE

This company reduces premiums by 5 percent on all coverage from ages 50 to 54 in most states. From 55 to 69, you'll get a 10 percent discount; from 70 on, you get only a 5 percent reduction once more. Take a defensive-driving course and almost everywhere you'll be entitled to an additional 5 to 15 percent off.

PROGRESSIVE

This large insurance company offers a free 24-hour automobile insurance rate comparison service to help you decide on the best rate for you, discounts or not. If you dial 800-AUTO-PRO, you will get rate comparisons for up to four different major insurance companies, including Progressive, in your state.

PRUDENTIAL

Prudential gives drivers ages 50 through 54 a discount of about 10 percent in most states, 15 percent for ages 55 through 64, 10 percent for ages 65 through 74. You'll get an additional discount of 5 to 10 percent when you complete a defensive-driving course.

On homeowner insurance, there's a 5 percent Mature Homeowner Credit if one owner on the policy is 55 or more.

KEEP AN INVENTORY OF HOUSEHOLD GOODS

A free booklet, *Nonbusiness Disaster, Casualty and Theft Loss Workbook* (Publication No. 584), available from the Internal Revenue Service, is designed to help you determine the amount of a casualty or theft loss deduction for household goods and personal property. You use the booklet to list your possessions on a room-by-room basis, with space to record the number of items, date acquired, cost, value, and amount of loss. It is not easy to make a complete inventory of your possessions, but it is easier than trying to remember all those details after a theft or fire. Pick the booklet up at your local IRS office or call 800-TAX-FORM (800-829-3676).

STATE FARM

Buy automobile insurance from State Farm and you'll get a 5 percent discount on certain coverages if you are 55 or more.

TRAVELERS

With this insurance company (now merged with Aetna's property and casualty division), the discount you get across the board on automobile coverage varies according to your age. From ages 50 through 64, the discount amounts to 10 to 15 percent depending on the state in which you live. From 65 through 74, it's 15 to 20 percent; and over 75, 5 to 10 percent. Completing a defensive-driving course will add another 5 percent discount in some states for those over 55. The vehicle must be used essentially for pleasure and no driver may be under 25 years of age.

On homeowner insurance, you will get 10 to 20 percent reductions on premiums, depending on the state, when you are 50 or more.

HOW TO FIND LOCAL ELDER SERVICES

For information about housing, home health services, adult day care centers, legal assistance, or other kinds of services for older people, call the Eldercare Locator at 800-677-1116. This nationwide governmental resource for elderly people or their caregivers will help you find an appropriate agency or program in your area. Call between 9 A.M. and 8 P.M. (Eastern Time) Monday through Friday and explain the problem. Be sure you know the name, address, and zip code of the person needing help.

BANKING

Many banks offer special incentives and services to their mature customers, including free checks; elimination of monthly service charges; no-fee traveler's checks, cashier's checks, and money orders; and free safe-deposit boxes. All banks and state regulations are different so you must do some comparison shopping to be sure you are receiving the best deal available in your community.

LEGAL ASSISTANCE

Call upon your local area senior agency, which is required by law to provide some legal assistance to older citizens. Yours may help you untangle some puzzling legal problems or, at least, tell you what services are available to you. Or contact your local bar association for information about referrals or pro bono programs. In some states, AARP members may get legal advice through the organization's Legal Services Network.

18

Volunteer for Great Experiences

If, perhaps for the first time in your life, you have time, expertise, talent, and energy to spare, consider volunteering your services to organizations that could use your help. There is plenty of significant work waiting for you. If you are looking for a good match between your abilities and a program that needs them, take a look at the programs described here, all of them specifically seeking the experience and enthusiasm of mature adults.

But, first, keep in mind:

When you file your federal income tax, you may be allowed to deduct unreimbursed expenses incurred while volunteering your services. These usually include program fees and reasonable costs for transportation, parking, tolls, meals, lodging, and uniforms. You may not be able to deduct all of your travel expenses, meals, and lodging when you spend a significant amount of personal or vacation time before, during, or after a service program, or if you get benefit from your service, such as academic credit.

AARP VOLUNTEER TALENT BANK

If you want to help others, get in touch with AARP's Volunteer Talent Bank program, which puts people and work together. Many AARP programs are offered locally and conducted by volunteers in your own neighborhood. When you register, you'll be asked to complete a questionnaire about your experience, skills, and special interests, and this is matched with volunteer opportunities within the organization or by referral to other agencies in your community.

For information: To get the address of the AARP chapter nearest you, contact AARP Volunteer Talent Bank, 601 E St. NW, Washington, DC 20049; 800-424-3410 or 202-434-AARP.

ELDERHOSTEL SERVICE PROGRAMS

Elderhostel Service Programs tap the experience and expertise of older adults (55 or over) in short-term volunteer projects in the U.S., Canada, and throughout the world. Teams of hostelers are paired with nonprofit organizations for a wide variety of service activities, from teaching English to ecological research, conservation work, working with special-needs children, assisting in archaeological digs, and helping to build affordable housing.

Currently more than 83 institutions and organizations—far too many to list here—are collaborating with

Elderhostel to put mature Americans, retired or not, to work for one to three weeks per session. These include such diverse groups as Habitat for Humanity, Oceanic Society Expeditions, the U.S. Forest Service, Global Volunteers, Pueblo Community College, Hole in the Woods Ranch, the Center for Bioacoustics, Chicago's Museum of Science and Industry, Grand Canyon National Park, and many more.

No prior experience or training is required, and the fee you must pay to participate, which includes full room and board, equipment, round-trip airfare (in most cases), and social and cultural events, is moderate.

For information: Elderhostel, 75 Federal St., Boston, MA 02110; 617-426-7788. In Canada: Elderhostel Canada, 5 Cataraqui St., Kingston, ON K7K 1Z7; 613-530-2222.

FAMILY FRIENDS

A national program sponsored by the National Council on Aging, Family Friends recruits volunteers over the age of 55 to work with children with disabilities, chronic illnesses, or other problems in many locations around the country. The volunteers act as caring grandparents, helping the families in whatever ways they can, mostly dealing with children at home but occasionally in hospitals. They are asked to serve at least four hours a week and to commit themselves to the program for at least a year. Volunteers are reimbursed for expenses incurred.

The local projects are funded by the federal government, corporations, foundations, and local, county, city, or state governments.

For information: Family Friends Resource Center, 409

Third St. SW, Washington, DC 20024; 202-479-6675.

FOSTER GRANDPARENTS PROGRAM

This federal program sponsored by the government's national volunteer agency offers gratifying volunteer work to thousands of income-eligible men and women 60 and over, in communities all over the 50 states, Puerto Rico, the Virgin Islands, and the District of Columbia. The volunteers, who receive 40 hours of preservice orientation and training and four hours a month of in-service training, work with children who have special needs—boarder babies; troubled children; handicapped, severely retarded, abandoned, delinquent, abused, hospitalized, addicted, forlorn children who are desperate for love, care, and attention and do not get it from their families. Volunteers may work in hospitals, schools, homes, day-care programs, or residential centers.

Volunteers, who must be in good health although they may be handicapped, serve 20 hours a week. For this, they receive, aside from the immense satisfaction, a small tax-free annual stipend, a transportation allowance, hot meals while at work, accident and liability insurance, and annual physicals.

For information: Contact your local Foster Grandparents program, or the Corporation for National Service, 1201 New York Ave. NW, Washington, DC 20525; 800-424-8867.

INTERNATIONAL EXECUTIVE SERVICE CORPS

IESC, organized and directed by U.S. business executives, is a nonprofit organization that recruits retired, highly skilled executives and technical advisors in order to assist businesses in the developing nations. It is funded by the U.S. Agency for International Development (AID), overseas clients and foreign governments, and many American corporations.

After being briefed on the country and the client, volunteer executives travel overseas—with their spouses, if they wish—for projects that generally last two to three months. IESC pays for the couple's travel expenses and provides a per diem allowance.

For information: International Executive Service Corps, 333 Ludlow St., Stamford, CT 06902; 800-243-4372 or 203-967-6000.

HOW TO HELP THE ENVIRONMENT

Environmental Alliance for Senior Involvement (EASI) is designed to tap the talents, knowledge, experience, and enthusiasm of older environmental activists. Together with local and national senior and environmental organizations such as AARP, RSVP, the EPA, the National Council on Aging, World Wildlife Fund, and National Wildlife Federation, volunteers work to preserve and restore the natural world for future generations. Current projects include pollution control, water source protection, solar energy installations, and radon identification.

For information: EASI, 8733 Old Dumfries Rd., Catlett, VA 20119; 540-788-3274.

NATIONAL EXECUTIVE SERVICE CORPS

This nonprofit organization performs a unique service: it helps other nonprofit organizations solve their problems by providing retired executives with extensive corporate and professional experience to serve as volunteer consultants. Its services are offered in five basic areas—education, health, the arts, social services, and religion—and the assistance covers everything from organizational structure and financial systems to marketing and funding strategy. Volunteers' expenses are covered.

For information: National Executive Service Corps, 257 Park Ave. South, New York, NY 10010; 212-529-6660.

NATIONAL PARK SERVICE

If you love the outdoors and have the time, volunteer to work for the National Park Service as a VIP (Volunteers in Parks). VIPs are not limited to over-50s, but a good portion of them are retired people with time, expertise, talent, and interest in forests and wilderness. You may work a few hours a week or a month, seasonally or full-time, and may or may not—depending on the park—wear a uniform or get reimbursed for out-of-pocket expenses. The job possibilities range from working at an information desk to serving as a guide, maintaining trails, driving a shuttle bus, painting fences, designing computer programs, patrolling trails, making wildlife counts, writing visitor brochures, and preparing park events.

For information: Contact the VIP coordinator at the national park where you would like to volunteer and request an application. Or, write to Volunteer Coordinator, National Park Service, 18th and C Sts. NW, Ste. 3045, Washington, DC 20240; 202-565-1060.

NATIONAL TRUST WORKING HOLIDAYS

Britain's National Trust runs hundreds of "working holidays" in England, Wales, and Northern Ireland, inviting volunteers to exchange work for an interesting and low-cost holiday. The National Trust, which oversees Britain's historic and environmental treasures, organizes small groups of people to lend a hand for one-week sessions in such tasks as restoring historic buildings, clearing ponds, or maintaining footpaths. Most programs accept anybody over the age of 18, but several—the Oak Plus Projects—are reserved for enthusiasts between 50 and 70 who are willing to tackle outdoor work.

Lodging is in dormitory-style base camps and the work is paced to allow ample time to relax, take in the local attractions, or go for a stroll.

For information: The National Trust, PO Box 84, Cirencester, Glos, GL7 1ZP, England.

PEACE CORPS

It may surprise you to learn that the Peace Corps is a viable choice for idealists of any age. Eighty is the upper age limit for acceptance into the Peace Corps, and since its beginning in 1961 thousands of Senior Volunteers have brought their talents and experience to almost 100 countries all over the world. To become a Senior Volunteer, you must be a U.S. citizen and meet basic legal and medical criteria. Some assignments require a college or technical-school degree or an experience equivalent. Married couples are eligible and will be assigned together. Service is typically for two years.

What you get in return is the chance to travel, an unforgettable living experience in a foreign land, basic expenses, and housing, plus technical, language, and cultural training. You'll also have a chance to use your expertise constructively in fields such as agriculture, engineering, math/science, home economics, education, skilled trades, forestry and fisheries, and community development.

For information: Peace Corps, 1990 K St. NW, Washington, DC 20526; 800-424-8580.

RSVP (RETIRED AND SENIOR VOLUNTEER PROGRAM)

RSVP, an organization that receives funding, support, and technical assistance from the Corporation for National Service, the federal domestic volunteer agency, and functions under the auspices of local service organizations, matches the interests and abilities of men and women over 55 with part-time volunteer opportunities in their own communities. RSVP volunteers may be assigned to work in schools, libraries, courts, day-care centers, crisis centers, hospitals, nursing homes, or economic development agencies. You may get involved in tax aid, home repair, counseling, refugee assistance, home visitation, adult education, or whatever other services are needed in your area. You will serve without pay but may be reimbursed for or provided with transportation and other expenses. You may work for only several hours a week or many more than that if you wish.

For information: Contact your local or regional RSVP office or Corporation for National Service, 1201 New York Ave. NW, Washington, DC 20525; 800-424-8867.

SENIOR COMPANIONS

Senior Companions are income-eligible Americans 60 or over who volunteer four hours a day, five days a week, to provide services and companionship for the homebound, helping them maintain their independence. In a program funded and supported by the Corporation for National Service and by local agencies, the volunteers help other people cope with life. For example, they assist disabled veterans, recovering mental patients, Alzheimer's patients, the blind, recovering substance abusers, men and women recuperating from major surgery or illnesses, and those who are in chronic frail health.

Although the volunteers are not paid, they receive a modest nontaxable stipend that does not affect Social Security eligibility, reimbursement for transportation and meals, on-duty insurance, and an annual physical exam.

For information: Corporation for National Service, 1201 New York Ave. NW, Washington, DC 20525; 800-424-8867.

SENIOR ENVIRONMENTAL EMPLOYMENT PROGRAM (SEE)

The SEE Program, administered by the Environmental Protection Agency (EPA), establishes grants to private non-profit organizations to recruit, hire, and pay experienced people over the age of 55 to help fight environmental problems. The recruits, who work part-time or full-time in EPA offices or in the field, are paid by the hour in jobs ranging from secretarial and clerical work to highly specialized positions. All are designed to assist the agency in protecting the environment and cleaning up America.

For information: Contact your regional EPA office or SEE Program, EPA, 401 M St. SW, Washington, DC 20460; 202-260-2574.

FORTY PLUS CLUBS

Offices in 20 cities throughout the United States comprise this nonprofit cooperative of unemployed executives, managers, and professionals, men and women, 40 years of age or more. Their objective is to help members conduct effective job searches and find new jobs. There is no paid staff. The members do all the work and help pay expenses by paying $500 upon acceptance and then $100 a month thereafter. They must commit themselves to attend weekly meetings and spend at least two days a week working at the club and assisting others in their search for work.

In return, members are helped to examine their career skills and define their goals, counseled on résumé writing and interview skills, helped to plan marketing strategy, and given job leads. They may also use the club as a base of operations, with phone answering and mail service, computers, and reference library.

Forty Plus Clubs exist at this writing in New York City and Buffalo, New York; Oakland, San Diego, San Jose, and Los Angeles (with a branch in Laguna Hills), California; Fort Collins, Colorado Springs, and Lakewood, Colorado; Columbus, Ohio; Dallas and Houston, Texas; Murray, Ogden, and Provo, Utah; Philadelphia, Pennsylvania; Bellevue, Washington; Washington, D.C.; St. Paul, Minnesota; and Honolulu, Hawaii.

For information: Addresses of the clubs and descriptive materials are available from Forty Plus of New York, 15 Park Row, New York, NY 10038; 212-233-6086.

THE SERVICE CORPS OF RETIRED EXECUTIVES

SCORE is a national organization of both active and retired professionals and business executives who offer their expertise free of charge to small businesses. SCORE counselors, who include lawyers, business executives, accountants, engineers, managers, journalists, and other specialists, provide management assistance and advice to small-business people who are going into business or who are already in business but need expert help.

With a current membership of more than 12,000 men and women, SCORE has about 400 counseling locations all over the mainland United States as well as Puerto Rico, Guam, and the Virgin Islands. Funded and coordinated by the government's Small Business Administration, it is operated and administered by a staff and an elected board of volunteers.

For information: Contact your local U.S. Small Business Administration office or SCORE, 409 Third St. SW, 4th floor, Washington, DC 20416; 800-634-0245 or 202-205-6762.

SERVICE OPPORTUNITIES FOR OLDER PEOPLE (SOOP)

SOOP, sponsored by the Mennonite Board of Missions and the Mennonite Central Committee Canada, provides a way for older people to contribute their experience and skills in a variety of locations throughout the U.S. and Canada. You may sign up for two weeks or up to a year, living at the site and working to help others in need in whatever way you can, from teaching, building, and child care to homemaking, farming, and administering. Once you decide on the kind of work and time commitment you prefer, you make plans with a location coordinator for your assignment and housing. Volunteers pay for their own travel, food, and lodging.

For information: Mennonite Board of Missions, PO Box 370, Elkhart, IN 46515; 219-294-7523.

SHEPHERD'S CENTERS OF AMERICA (SCA)

An interfaith, nonprofit organization of older adults who volunteer their skills to help seniors in their communities, SCA has about 90 centers in 26 states. Supported by Catholic, Jewish, and Protestant congregations as well as businesses and foundations, the centers operate many programs designed to enable older people to remain in their own homes as active participants in community life. They also encourage intergenerational interaction. Centers offer such in-home services as Telephone Visitors, Family Friends, Meals on Wheels, Handyhands Service, and Respite Care, all provided mostly by volunteers. Programs at the centers include other services, day trips, classes, and courses as well as support groups and referrals. Membership is open to anyone over the age of 55.

For information: Shepherd's Centers of America, 1 W. Armour, Ste. 201, Kansas City, MO 64111; 800-547-7073.

VOLUNTEER GRANDPARENTS SOCIETY

The objective of this nonprofit organization in Canada is to match volunteer grandparents with families with children between the ages of 3 and 12 who have no accessible grandparents. The volunteers, who are not paid and do not commit to a contract or specific hours, establish a relationship of mutual enjoyment, support, and caring and become part of an extended family. They are also placed in school classrooms, serving as a supportive presence for the children. Applicants are interviewed and carefully screened, and matches are based on compatibility as well as on geographic proximity. The organization, which originated in 1973 in Vancouver, is expanding with the development of programs in 10 centers across Canada in addition to several already in British Columbia.

For information: Volunteer Grandparents, #3, 1734 W. Broadway, Vancouver, BC V6J 1Y1.

JOB PROGRAM FOR OLDER WORKERS

Senior Community Service Employment Program (SCSEP), a federally funded program, recruits unemployed low-income men and women over the age of 55, assesses their employment strengths, and hires them for paid jobs in community-service positions. At the same time, the enrollees begin training in new job skills and receive such help as counseling, physical examinations, group meetings, and job fairs while the agency tries to match them with permanent jobs in the private sector. If you qualify and are looking for a paying position, this agency is worth a try.

For information: SCSEP, National Council on the Aging, 409 Third St. SW, Washington, DC 20024; 202-479-1200. Or contact your local, county, or state Office for the Aging.

VOLUNTEERS IN TECHNICAL ASSISTANCE

VITA provides another avenue for helping developing countries. A nonprofit international organization, VITA provides volunteer experts who respond—usually by direct correspondence—to technical inquiries from people in these nations who need assistance in such areas as small-business development, energy applications, agriculture, reforestation, water supply and sanitation, and low-cost housing. Its volunteers also perform other services such as project planning, translations, publications, marketing strategies, evaluations, and technical reports and often become on-site consultants.

There is no minimum age, but you must be retired to serve. If you become a volunteer, you will not be paid, but you will be reimbursed for your travel and living expenses. *For information:* Volunteers in Technical Assistance, 1600 Wilson Blvd., Ste. 500, Arlington, VA 22209; 703-276-1800.

VOLUNTEER PROGRAMS IN ISRAEL

ACTIVE RETIREES IN ISRAEL (ARI)

Sponsored by B'nai B'rith International, ARI is a volunteer work program for people who are 50, in good health, and members of B'nai B'rith. Volunteers pay for the opportunity to live in the resort city of Netanya and work in the mornings for one or two months in hospitals, forests, kibbutzim, schools, and facilities for the elderly and the handicapped. Afternoons are spent learning Hebrew, while the evenings include concerts, discussion groups, and cultural activities. Guided tours of the country are part of the program. Optional trips to Eilat are available as add-ons to your stay.

For information: ARI, B'nai B'rith Israel Commission, 1640 Rhode Island Ave. NW, Washington, DC 20036; 800-500-6533 or 202-857-6580.

JEWISH NATIONAL FUND

To qualify for the JNF Canadian American Active Retirees in Israel, a two-month winter program sponsored by the Jewish National Fund, you must be over 50 and in good physical and mental health. Your time will be spent working five mornings a week, tending the JNF national forests and, in addition, working at a choice of other jobs. Some volunteers choose to contribute their time in schools, hospitals, homes for the aged, army bases, universities, or kibbutzim, while others assist local craftspeople or archaeologists. Afternoons are devoted to planned activities, including Hebrew lessons, and evenings are devoted to socializing. Included is a tour of the country and time in Jerusalem.

For information: JNF CA-ARI Program, Missions Dept., 42 E. 69th St., New York, NY 10021; 800-223-7787 or 212-879-9300, ext. 283.

VOLUNTEERS FOR ISRAEL

In this volunteer work-and-cultural program for adults 18 and older in Israel, you'll put in eight-hour days for three weeks, sleep in a segregated dormitory, and work in small groups at a reserve or supply military base, doing whatever needs doing most at that moment. You may serve in supply, warehousing, or maintenance of equipment or in social services in hospitals. You'll wear an army uniform with a "Civilian Volunteer" patch. Board, room, and other expenses are free, but you must pay for your own partially subsidized airfare.

For information: Volunteers for Israel, 330 West 42nd St., 16th floor, New York, NY 10036-6902; 212-643-4848.

FOR JOB HUNTERS

If you're over 40 and in the market for a job but don't know where to start looking for one, hook up with **Operation ABLE**, a nonprofit organization affiliated with agencies that will help match you with a likely employer. You're in luck if you live in Chicago, where there are four regional offices. In addition, there is a network of independent ABLE-like organizations, modeled after the original, in several other cities, including New York, Boston, Denver, Los Angeles, Little Rock, Lincoln, and Washington, D.C.

Operation ABLE tries every which way to get you into the working world. It provides job counseling, on-the-job training, group training activities, and individual career assessment and guidance; teaches job-hunting skills; matches older workers with employers; operates a pool of temporaries; and offers myriad other services.

For information: Operation ABLE, 180 N. Wabash Ave., Chicago, IL 60601; 312-782-3335.

WINTER AND SPRING IN NETANYA PROGRAMS

Hadassah's Winter in Netanya (WIN) and Springtime in Netanya (SPIN) programs send volunteers to Israel for one or two months to work, study, and absorb Israeli culture. For a month in December, for two months in January and February, or for a month in the spring, American participants live in a four-star hotel in Netanya, a Mediterranean resort town 20 miles north of Tel Aviv. Here the volunteer workers, most of them retirees, spend their mornings working at the local hospital, tutoring schoolchildren in English, packing supplies for the Israel Defense Forces, pruning and planting trees, visiting senior centers, painting murals, or doing carpentry. Afternoons are devoted to optional Hebrew lessons and sight-seeing tours, while evenings are reserved for social and cultural events.

For information: Hadassah, 50 West 58th St., New York, NY 10019; 212-303-8133 or your local Hadassah chapter.

AARP WORKS

A series of seven three-hour career-planning workshops for men and women over 50 who are seeking employment, **AARP Works** is offered year-round all over the country. Led by volunteer teams and community agencies, the workshops focus on such subjects as interview skills, job-search strategies, effective resumes, age discrimination, short-term employment, self-assessment of skills, and work experience. A fee of $20 is charged for the series.

For information: Contact your local AARP area office. For the location of the nearest area office, call AARP Member Services at 800-424-3410.

19

The Over-50 Organizations and What They Can Do for You

When you consider that there are more people in this country over the age of 55 than there are children in elementary and high schools, you can see why we have powerful potential to influence what goes on around here. As the demographic discovery of the times, a group that controls most of the nation's disposable income, we've become a prime marketing target. And, just like any other large group of people, we've got plenty of needs.

A number of organizations in the United States and Canada have been formed in recent years to act as advocates for the mature population and to provide us with special programs as well as opportunities to spend our money on their products or services. Here is a brief rundown on them and what they have to offer you. You may want to join more than one of them so you can get the best of each.

271

AARP (AMERICAN ASSOCIATION OF RETIRED PERSONS)

At age 50 you are eligible to join AARP, the extensive non-profit organization that serves as an advocate for the older generation, offers a vast array of services and programs, and sells many kinds of insurance. With more than 32 million members, it is one of the most effective lobbying groups in the country. You do not have to be retired to join. Its newsletter *AARP Bulletin* and magazine *Modern Maturity* go to more homes than any other publications in the U.S. For an annual membership fee of $8 (and that includes a spouse), AARP offers so many benefits that you are likely to stop reading before the end of the list. But here are some of them:

- Group health insurance, life insurance, auto insurance, homeowner's insurance, mobile-home insurance
- Discounts on hotels, motels, auto rentals, and sight-seeing
- A mail-order pharmacy service that delivers prescription and nonprescription drugs
- A motoring plan that includes emergency road and towing services, trip planning, and other benefits
- A national advocacy and lobbying program at all levels of government to develop legislative priorities and represent the interests of older people
- More than 4,000 local chapters with their own activities and volunteer projects
- The Volunteer Talent Bank, which matches you with volunteer opportunities in your community
- A series of employment planning workshops called AARP Works for older job hunters

- Special programs in a wide range of areas such as consumer affairs, legal counseling, financial information, housing, health advocacy, voter education, employment planning, independent living, disability initiatives, grandparent information, and public benefits
- Tax-Aide, a program conducted in cooperation with the IRS that helps lower- and moderate-income members with their income tax returns
- 55 ALIVE/Mature Driving, a classroom course developed to refresh your driving skills and in many states help you qualify for lower auto insurance rates
- Free publications on many subjects relevant to your life

For information: AARP, 601 E St. NW, Washington, DC 20049; 800-424-3410 or 202-434-AARP.

CARP (CANADIAN ASSOCIATION OF RETIRED PERSONS)

Singles or couples may join CARP, a national nonprofit association of 320,000 Canadians aged 50 and over, retired or not, for $10 (Canadian) a year or $25 for three years. Like AARP, this organization offers discount rates on many good things, such as hotel rooms, car rentals, out-of-country health insurance, extended health and dental plans, car or home insurance plans; and special travel discounts. It publishes an award-winning lively and informative newspaper, *CARPNews*, six times a year and sponsors national and provincial advocacy programs on issues of concern to older people—for example, pensions, health care, and protection against scams and frauds. Look for CARP's free financial seminars held frequently throughout the country. *For information:* CARP, 27 Queen St. East, Ste. 1304,

Toronto, ON M5C 2M6; 800-363-9736 or 416-383-8748.

CANADIAN SNOWBIRD ASSOCIATION

CSA is an organization formed to represent the interests of Canadian snowbirds, people who flee the winter snow for the sun and palm trees of the U.S. southern states. As their advocate and lobbying group, CSA addresses issues of concern to Canadian seniors such as health care, absentee voting rights, cross-border problems, residency requirements, U.S. tax laws for Canadians wintering abroad, and estate tax rules on Canadian-owned vacation property in the U.S. And it endorses travel insurance as well as out-of-country health insurance.

Membership costs $10 (single) and $15 (couple) per year, and benefits include a magazine, group travel offerings, an automobile club, a currency-exchange program, mail-order pharmacy services, a discount on membership in AOL, discounted prescriptions and telephone calls, discounts on hotel room rates, and social gatherings in popular snowbird locations such as Florida and Arizona.

For information: Canadian Snowbird Association, 180 Lesmill Rd., North York, ON M3B 2T5; 800-265-3200.

CATHOLIC GOLDEN AGE

A Catholic nonprofit organization that is concerned with issues affecting older citizens, such as health care, housing, and Social Security benefits, CGA has well over a million members and more than 200 chapters throughout the country. It offers many good things to its members, who must be over 50. These include spiritual benefits, such as masses and prayers worldwide, and practical benefits, such as dis-

counts on hotels, campgrounds, car rentals, and prescriptions. Other offerings include group insurance plans, pilgrimage and group travel programs, and an automobile club. Membership costs $8 a year or $19 for three years.
For information: Catholic Golden Age, 430 Penn Ave., Scranton, PA 18503; 800-836-5699.

MATURE OUTLOOK

Sponsored by Sears, the country's largest retailer, Mature Outlook is a discount club for people who have turned 50. Its 750,000 members are entitled to discounts on products and services in all Sears stores in the U.S. and Canada. When you join for a fee of $19.95 a year (includes you and your spouse), you receive $100 in Sears money coupons to spend as you like. Other benefits of membership include membership in a hotel discount program, a dining plan that can save you money in restaurants worldwide, travel discounts, discounts on car rentals, and reductions on the cost of eye examinations and eyeglasses. In addition, you receive six issues a year of *Mature Outlook Magazine,* a good read that also keeps you informed about upcoming opportunities for savings.
For information: Mature Outlook, PO Box 10448, Des Moines, IA 50306; 800-336-6330.

NATIONAL COUNCIL OF SENIOR CITIZENS

An advocacy organization, NCSC lobbies on the local, state, and national level for legislation benefiting older Americans. With about five million members, it has carried on many campaigns concerning Medicare, housing, health care, Social Security, and other relevant programs.

Although NCSC's major focus is its legislative program, it also has a local club network, social events, prescription discounts, group rates on supplemental health insurance, automobile insurance, and travel discounts, plus a newspaper that keeps you up to date on all of the above. Membership costs $13 a year or $33 for three years.

For information: National Council of Senior Citizens, 8403 Colesville Rd., Ste. 1200, Silver Springs, MD 20910; 800-333-7212 or 301-578-8800.

NATIONAL ASSOCIATION FOR RETIRED CREDIT UNION PEOPLE

Obviously, not everybody can join this club, but those who do—past and present members of a credit union who are at least 50 years old or retired—will get some good benefits. These include a magazine called *Prime Times*, a newsletter, car-rental discounts, Medicare supplement insurance, pharmacy discounts, lodging discounts at some hotels and campgrounds, and a motor club. Also, discounted travel packages and tours.

For information: NARCUP, PO Box 391, Madison, WI 53701; 800-937-2644, ext. 6070, or 608-232-6070.

NATIONAL ASSOCIATION OF RETIRED FEDERAL EMPLOYEES

As you can probably gather, this is an association of federal retirees and their families. Its primary mission is to protect the earned benefits of retired federal employees via its lobbying program in Washington. Members receive a monthly magazine and are entitled to discounts and special services. *For information:* NARFE, 1533 New Hampshire Ave. NW, Washington, DC 20036; 800-627-3394 or 202-234-0832.

OLDER WOMEN'S LEAGUE

OWL is a national nonprofit organization with local chapters dedicated to achieving economic, political, and social equality for older women. Anyone, any age, may join. OWL provides educational materials, training for citizen advocates, and informative publications dealing with the important issues—such as Social Security, health care, retirement benefits, employment discrimination—facing women as they grow older. Annual dues: $25.
For information: Older Women's League, 666 11th St. NW, Washington, DC 20001; 800-825-3695 or 202-783-6686.

NATIONAL ALLIANCE OF SENIOR CITIZENS

This national lobbying organization with over 100,000 members has a decidedly conservative tilt-to-the-right bias, so people with middle-of-the-road or liberal views would not feel too much at home here. It works to influence national policy "on key issues of great importance to America and her future." As a member you receive newsletters and benefits that include group insurance, prescription discounts, discounts on car rentals, lodgings, moving expenses, and an automobile club.
For information: National Alliance of Senior Citizens, 1744 Riggs Pl. NW, Washington, DC 20009; 202-986-0117.

NATIONAL EDUCATION ASSOCIATION–RETIRED

With a membership of more than 155,000 retired education employees from teachers to school bus drivers, NEA–Retired acts as an advocate for their special interests such as pensions and health care and supports public education through legislative lobbying as well as reading programs, mentoring, and intergenerational activities. Among its benefits of membership are life, health, disability, and casualty insurance programs; savings and investment plans; credit and loan programs; and discounts, educational guides, and a bimonthly magazine. Join for $15 a year or $100 for life plus local dues that vary by state.

For information: NEA–Retired, 1201 16th St. NW, Washington, DC 20036; 202-822-7149.

GRAY PANTHERS

A national organization of intergenerational activists, the Gray Panthers work on multiple issues that include peace, jobs for all, antidiscrimination (ageism, sexism, racism), family security, the environment, campaign reform, and the United Nations. They are active in more than 50 local networks across the United States in their efforts to promote their goal of advancing social justice. For annual membership dues of $20, members receive a bimonthly newsletter, which is also available by subscription.

For information: Gray Panthers, 2025 Pennsylvania Ave. NW, Ste. 821, Washington, DC 20006; 800-280-5362 or 202-466-3132.

THE RETIRED OFFICERS ASSOCIATION

This group is open to anyone who has been a commissioned or warrant officer in the seven U.S. uniformed services. Members receive lobbying representation on Capitol Hill and an excellent magazine that features articles on matters of special interest to them. They may also take advantage of a number of benefits, including discounts on car rentals and motel lodgings, a travel program with "military fares" to many overseas destinations, sports tournaments, a mail-order prescription program, group health and life insurance plans, and a car lease-purchase plan. TROA also has many autonomous local chapters with their own activities and membership fees.

For information: The Retired Officers Association, 201 N. Washington St., Alexandria, VA 22314; 800-245-8762 or 703-549-2311.

UNITED SENIORS ASSOCIATION

The United Seniors Association fights for "less government regulation and lower taxes" for seniors. Organized to help stop a national health care plan, its mission is to lobby Congress for its conservative agenda and to get its point of view known via the media, position papers, and a newsletter. Membership costs $5 a year per household.

For information: USA, Inc., 3900 Jermantown Rd., Ste. 450, Fairfax, VA 22030; 800-890-1166 or 703-359-6500.

Index